PRAISE FOR *T*

MW00629605

"The fascinating part about Melinda Brody's Mystery Shopping horror stories is not just that they are true but also that they are commonplace. This book is a must read for any Sales Manager interested in developing an extraordinary sales team."

—JOE CATANZARITI
Regional Sales Trainer
Lennar Corporation

"Sales agents and sales managers will enjoy this book, as I did. Great tips on how to have a successful mystery shop and sell new homes using a sales process, plus entertaining stories on what to do and what NOT to do!"

—MARY JANE MCNAUGHT
Sales & Marketing Manager, Central Florida
D.R. Horton, America's Builder

"*They Said What??!!* is just what the sales manager ordered! Not only does Melinda offer three decades worth of hard lessons learned through mystery shopping, she does so in an extremely entertaining and educational way. Read this book, apply Melinda's principles, and sell more homes. It couldn't be easier."

—JOHN A. PALUMBO
Author of *Selling at the Top, Middle, or Bottom of Any Market*

"*They Said What??!!* is a fun and interesting read right from the start. The book encapsulates everything that could go wrong, and Melinda Brody turns that into instruction on what should go right. Enjoy the book, but more importantly USE the book."

—JEFF SHORE
Sales Trainer, Author & Speaker

"*They Said What*" is one of those rare books that entertains as it educates, using both bad and good examples of selling techniques to teach the reader how to be a better new home sales counselor. Having led sales teams from 50 reps to 450, I can honestly say Melinda's book is a great read for builders of all sizes."

—LEE DARNOLD
Chief Marketing Officer/Vice President of Sales
Orleans Homes

"Shocking, funny and educational, this book has it all! If you're a sales agent or new home sales manager. "*They Said What??!!*" should be required reading. You will learn how to become a top producing agent from the good, bad, and even the ugly examples in this book. I couldn't put it down!"

—MEREDITH OLIVER
Internet Sales & Marketing Expert
Creating WOW Communications

THEY SAID WHAT??!!

Behind the Scenes of *25,000* Undercover Video Mystery Shops

MELINDA BRODY

August 2013

Melinda Brody

ISBN 978-0-615-85540-0

www.MelindaBrody.com

Book design, layout and interior by Jerry Dorris, AuthorSupport

DEDICATION

"They Said What??!!" is dedicated to Joe Brody,
who encouraged me to be an entrepreneur because
"You can always get a job."

I miss you every day, Dad.

Table of Contents

INTRODUCTION

"They Said What??!!" is different from any other book you've ever read or will read about selling new homes. How? You're going to learn how to do everything wrong. Yes, wrong! You get to step into the shoes of Sales Agents (SA's) who were a total debacle. And by experiencing their mistakes (and probably enjoying many laughs along the way), you'll then learn how to do your job far better and make your sales soar. If you manage a team of sales agents, the principles in this book will raise the performance level of your entire sales team. Not just a little, but a lot!

For almost 30 years, I've provided undercover video shopping services to the homebuilding industry. I've had the unique and extraordinary opportunity to video more than 25,000 (and still counting) onsite salespeople and I've seen just about every kind of presentation imaginable. Some have been good, some have been so-so, some have been bad, and some have been downright awful. In the process, I've learned the best techniques and the most common mistakes. In *"They Said What??!!"* I pass these lessons on to you.

Excellent techniques and consistent practice lead to outstanding success. Champion golfer Tiger Woods knows this better than most. Tiger continuously watches videos to improve every part of his game and he practices, practices, practices. Use this book in a similar way to achieve greater success in your field of new home sales.

In chapter 1, I begin by sharing some background about me, and then I dig into the value and benefits of video mystery shopping. Chapters 2 through 11 teach selling principles drawn from practical experience. Chapters 1 through 11 each start with a true shop story that will have you saying, *"They Said What??!!"* Chapter 11 ties everything together and offers a word of encouragement. Chapter 12 is more *"They Said What??!!"* stories! The surprise ending in chapter 12 is meant to be just that — a surprise; don't peek ahead!

The principles in *"They Said What??!!"* will make you far more successful than you are today. I've applied them and I've seen thousands of other industry professionals apply them. In fact, one SA not only did such a terrific job with her prospect using these principles and sold a home but the prospect turned out to be a shopper! If you read and practice the skills in this book, I promise 100% that you will **SELL MORE HOMES!**

CHAPTER 1

I Can Identify With You

It was an extremely hot day. I asked to see a one-bedroom model apartment. The leasing agent said, "Sure, let's go." No registration card. No discovery questions. She took me on an Olympic sprint…swung open the door to the air conditioned comfort of the model…and pushed us both inside. As I was catching my breath, the leasing agent said, "Here it is, take a look!" I looked around. Then she asked, "Well, what do ya think?" I answered, "Looks pretty nice." We continued our sprint…back to the leasing office — in silence. She handed me her business card. I attempted to smile and she said, "Have a nice day."

I'm the leasing agent in this story. It was July 1977.

Let me back up just a few months, to March 1977. I had been out of college for about a year, and I was eager to start a new career and a new life. But with only a sociology degree and no desire to go to graduate school, my choices were limited. The weather didn't help my spirits. It was freezing and snowing in Trenton, New Jersey, where I lived at the time, one of the coldest winters on record.

One day my phone rang. The cheery voice on the other end belonged to a friend from high school. "Come live with me down here in Orlando. Volleyball by the pool. Sun. Beach. Palm trees." I was on the auto train within a week.

My first few months in Orlando I played tourist. When July rolled around, it was time to get serious. My next hurdle was to find work. My friend suggested that I get a job as an apartment leasing agent. A nearby apartment community was looking for a leasing agent who would also serve as part-time social director. Fond memories of sorority parties came flooding back. I thought, "This is a job I can do!" I got the job.

My first week as a leasing agent was going well overall, but it did have some challenges. There's an expression, "It's so hot, you could fry an egg on the sidewalk." This is a true statement in Florida in July. My makeup streaked down my face. My clothes

2

were drenched from the humidity. Stockings were a required part of my uniform, so I avoided going outside as much as possible. I was glad to get out of the cold but I had moved to the opposite extreme. But, hey, it wasn't snowing, freezing, gray, and ugly. I was happy.

One day a gentleman walked in, nicely dressed in a three-piece pinstriped suit, and he asked to see a one-bedroom model apartment. And, well, I don't need to humiliate myself again. Just read the first paragraph in this chapter again.

I have to reminisce with you just a bit more. Maybe I can salvage myself a little, very little. There was a reason for the silence between me and the prospect as we walked back to the leasing office. All I could think about was, "It's so hot!" Also, I clearly remember the man's smile when he finally left my office because, in New York, where I grew up, anyone smiling and friendly is *up to something.*

After the man left, my manager, Mary Ann, motioned for me to come to her office. This was our conversation:

"Melinda, do you have any idea who that man was who just came in to see the model?"

"Nope," I replied.

"Does he look familiar?"

"Nope."

"Well, that was Ron Hall."

Deer-in-the-headlights look from me. "Who is Ron Hall?"

"Ron Hall is vice president of First Property Management, and you've just been shopped."

All I remember thinking at that moment was, "Shopping? That's something I do at Macy's or Dillards." And then, "This doesn't sound good. My short real estate career is over. It's back to Burger King."

When I sat down the following week and read the shopping evaluation report, I was shocked. I wondered, "Is this legal?" My score was minus 2. Not a zero or 1, but negative 2. It was all there in writing (video didn't exist yet): "Olympic sprint, no registration card, no discovery questions, no closing."

I reacted defensively, but it was all true. I was so embarrassed and ashamed that I vowed to never fail again. I was also angry, and I felt my anger was somewhat justified. I didn't know the criteria I was to be scored on. If I had been given the shopping report in advance and trained and coached on *how* to do the selling process correctly, the results would have been very, very different.

As you can see, I've made my share of mistakes, and I've learned from them. I so deeply believe in the value of video mystery shopping that I started my own company, Melinda Brody and Company, Inc., in 1986. My depth of experience gives me a unique understanding of both sides of the business of new home sales. This is why I'm so excited about helping you.

IS VIDEO MYSTERY SHOPPING SNEAKY?

Yes and no.

First, the "no." Most sales managers like video mystery shopping. They know how valuable it is for improving performance of the sales team and boosting sales.

Now the "yes," but only temporarily. Not surprisingly, most SA's have the opposite view. After all, who likes to see their mistakes captured on camera? Trust me, I understand the discomfort. I cringe when I watch videos of me giving speeches. That nasty camera never fails to make me look older and heavier than I really am. And why does it always zero in on my nervous giggle and awkward hand gestures?

One SA who got a score of 17 out of 100 on her first video shop told me, "I was so upset, I took a hammer and smashed my VHS tape to bits." However, when she thought through the feedback it provided, her outlook changed. She said, "I soon realized I learned more from that video shop than anything else in my career, and now I'm the sales trainer for my builder."

It's normal to be self-conscious watching a video of yourself. But if you're interested in selling more homes, video mystery shopping is your friend. Once you get past the discomfort and concentrate on your sales process, I promise that this powerful tool will help you grow more than you ever dreamed possible as a sales professional.

By the way, if you ever suspect that you're being mystery shopped, don't panic. Smile for the camera and turn on your best selling skills. If your suspicions are later confirmed, act surprised and enjoy your high score. If the prospect turns out to be legitimate, maybe you'll sell a home!

SHOPPING EVALUATION REPORT IS YOUR TICKET TO RECORD SALES

Most builders have their own shopping evaluation report. In case you don't have one, I've included my company's shopping report at the end of this chapter. This report is the key tool utilized throughout *"They Said What??!!"*

Each of the next 11 chapters relates to a section of the shopping evaluation report. As I discuss each section, I give you examples from our video files that illustrate the mistakes to avoid and the techniques you should use. I also provide principles that you can adopt to improve your performance.

If you're a sales manager, first give your sales team the shopping report. This makes them aware of what they're "supposed to do." Next, offer training and coaching to your SA's on how to flawlessly execute the steps on the shopping report. Third, test them onsite with a video mystery shop. Let them know in advance that you use mystery shopping. The only mystery should be the identity of the shopper.

The *"They Said What??!!"* Appendix includes Chapter Challenges, activities, and exercises to help implement ideas presented throughout the book.

Throughout *"They Said What??!!,"* including the Shopping Evaluation Report, I refer to the sales representative as the "sales agent" or "SA." The material in this book applies to both onsite sales agents who sell new homes and realtors. In an effort to not get too wordy, I use "SA" throughout the text, but please know that the information is applicable to **both** careers.

Let's get rolling and talk about the first step in the selling process: Approach/Introduction.

THEY SAID WHAT!!!!

Melinda Brody
AND COMPANY
Your One Stop Video Shop

Review Survey Questions (RSQ)		
Section	**Question**	**Potential**
Overview	Shopper Alias, phone number and email address used.	
Overview	Time shop began	
Overview	Length of shop in minutes	
Overview	Was "previsit" phone call made?	0
Overview	Please provide details.	
Overview	Did you have a positive first impression of the community?	0
Overview	Was the sales center easy to locate?	0
Overview	Did the office appear professional?	0
Overview	General Comments	
Recording	Provide URL to the recording	
Recording	Length of edited recording in minutes.	
Approach and Introduction	Did the SA welcome the prospect warmly and with enthusiasm?	1
Approach and Introduction	Did the SA initiate Introductions?	1
Approach and Introduction	Did the SA use the prospect's name more than twice during the visit?	1
Approach and Introduction	Did the SA offer the prospect refreshments?	1
Approach and Introduction	Was the registration card completed?	1
Approach and Introduction	Did the SA determine if the prospect had visited the website?	1
Qualify	Did the SA determine how much time the prospect had to spend on the visit?	1
Qualify	Did the SA determine the prospect's moving time frame?	1

8

Start in models

I Can Identify With You

SA clean care

Review Survey Questions (RSQ)		
Section	**Question**	**Potential**
Qualify	Did the SA determine the prospect's preferences in a layout?	1
Qualify	Did the SA determine the prospect's price range?	1
Qualify	Did the SA determine the prospect's family size?	1
Qualify	Did the SA determine if the prospect is renting or has a home to sell?	1
Qualify	Did the SA determine how the prospect heard of the community?	1
Qualify	Did the SA determine how long the prospect has been looking?	1
Qualify	Did the SA determine the prospect's moving motivation?	1
Qualify	Did the SA determine the prospect's line of work?	1
Community	Does this model center sell homes to be built on scattered lots?	0
Community	Did the SA determine the prospect's knowledge of the area?	1
Community	Did the SA offer information regarding schools, shopping and/or highways?	1
Community	Did the SA use visual aids to enhance the presentation?	1
Community	Did the SA discuss the community's amenities, if applicable?	1
Community	Did the SA offer information on HOA, CDD, or club membership fees, if applicable?	1
Community	Did the SA discuss the overview of community (# of homes, layout, etc,,,), if applicable?	1
Community	Did the SA trial close on community?	2
Builder	Did the SA tell the builder's story?	1
Builder	Did the SA point out the builder's uniqueness over the competition?	1
Builder	Did the SA offer information on the warranty?	1
Builder	Did the SA discuss the quality of construction?	1

"what's important to you . . . "

9

THEY SAID WHAT!!!!

Review Survey Questions (RSQ)		
Section	**Question**	**Potential**
Builder	Did the SA build value of the product?	1
Homes	Did the SA show the prospect available floor plans?	1
Homes	Did the SA demonstrate a model or available home?	3
Homes	Did the SA talk in terms of benefits as well as features?	1
Homes	Did the SA personalize the demonstration to the prospect's specific needs?	1
Homes	Did the SA discuss exterior features (landscaping, elevations, etc.)	1
Homes	Did the SA trial close on the home?	2
Location	Did the SA use the site map to show available locations, if applicable?	1
Location	Did the SA tour the locations with the prospect, if applicable?	3
Location	Did the SA use benefit selling for the location, if applicable?	1
Location	Did the SA trial close on the location, if applicable?	2
Objection	Describe the objection and how it was handled.	
Objection	Did the SA use empathy regarding the objection?	1
Objection	Did the SA clarify the prospect's concerns through questioning?	1
Objection	Did the SA offer solutions and/or suggestions to overcome the objection?	1
Objection	Did the SA make sure the prospect was satisfied with the solution?	1
Closing	Did the SA create a sense of urgency?	3
Closing	Did the SA review a wish list and discuss pricing with the prospect?	3
Closing	Did the SA fully explain the purchase procedure?	3
Closing	Did the SA determine if the prospect has spoken to a lender?	3

Section	Question	Potential
Review Survey Questions (RSQ)		
Closing	Did the SA offer information on the preferred lender(s)?	3
Closing	Did the SA determine when the prospect would be making a buying decision?	3
Closing	Did the SA proactively suggest moving forward?	5
Closing	Did SA determine why prospect is not ready to move forward?	3
Closing	Did the SA ask directly for a firm future appointment?	2
Sales Agent	Did the SA appear energetic and enthusiastic?	1
Sales Agent	Did the SA demonstrate a professional, courteous, friendly demeanor?	1
Sales Agent	Did the SA have an organized presentation?	1
Sales Agent	Did the SA seem in control of the sales process?	1
Sales Agent	Did the SA listen well?	1
Sales Agent	Did the SA attempt to build rapport with the prospect?	1
Sales Agent	Did the SA have good product knowledge?	1
Sales Agent	Did the SA handle traffic well (i.e. phone, multiple prospects, other visitors, etc.)	1
Sales Agent	Did the SA seem genuinely interested in the prospect?	1
Follow Up	Was follow up received?	5
Follow Up	Email follow-up.	
Follow Up	Date email follow-up was received.	
Follow Up	Phone follow-up.	
Follow Up	Date phone follow-up was received.	

CHAPTER 2

You Had Me At Hello

I arrived at the community at 10 a.m. Surprise, surprise, the agent wasn't there. I drove around the community and returned at 10:15 a.m. The agent greeted me and said, "Were you here yesterday?" I said that I was, but I saw he was busy with others and I decided to come back today. He said, "Yeah, I'm running a little late and slow today. I got ripped last night on too many beers. I probably should not have even driven myself to work today."

When I started my mystery shopping business in 1986, one of my first assignments was to shop a small builder in Orlando, Florida. This particular experience emphasized to me the critical point "hello" is in the sales process. As I entered the sales office, I heard muffled voices in the back of the model near the bedroom area. Suddenly the back door slammed. A short time later, a flustered female sales agent with mussed hair appeared. She greeted me while quickly buttoning her shirt. Oh, no! She was on a "date."

Business gradually picked up and I hired some shoppers to help me, one of whom was Pat. Pat went to a production builder community to shop a salesperson. She called me (on a pay phone!) in a panic: "I walked in and saw the salesperson on the floor....I think he's dead!"

"Why are you calling me?" I said. "Call 911!"

Pat called back about 15 minutes later: "The salesperson isn't dead. He was asleep!"

I mentioned this incident a few years ago at the Southeast Building Conference as an example of what not to do. A gentleman in the audience said, "Geez, I always take a nap in the master bedroom closet." He brought the house down. "Hey, I do the jokes around here!" I teased with the crowd.

APPROACH/INTRODUCTION IS THE FOUNDATION OF THE SALES PROCESS

The way you greet the prospect sets the stage for the entire visit. Period.

The goal of the Approach/Introduction is to break preoccupation and help your prospect relax and feel comfortable. In order to establish this kind of rapport, you must become the new home sales *counselor*.

As I cover the Approach/Introduction process, it will be helpful for you to keep in mind the questions on the shopping report. After the questions, I discuss those that need further explanation.

- Did the SA welcome the prospect warmly and with enthusiasm?
- Did the SA initiate introductions?
- Did the SA use the prospect's name more than twice during the visit?
- Did the SA offer the prospect refreshments?
- Did the SA complete the registration card?
- Did the SA determine if the prospect had visited the company's website?

THE GREETING SHOULD BE WARM AND FRIENDLY

Have you ever been snubbed by a salesperson who's supposed to be waiting on you? You know the kind of person I'm talking about. He's the guy who gives you a forced smile while continuing to talk on the phone, or the gal who doesn't even notice that you're waiting. It doesn't feel very good, does it?

Don't make these mistakes. Make it your goal to welcome prospects as you would welcome guests into your home. When they walk into your sales office, it's your opportunity and your responsibility to make them feel welcome, relaxed, and glad they came. Smile and warmly introduce yourself. Ask for, remember, and use their names.

These steps are so important, yet it's a common spot SA's mess up. Here are extracts from some of the appalling reports in our video mystery shop files:

....

The sales person greeted the shopper with a mouth full of food (just before he did the "slap-of-the-hands-to-remove-any-crumbs-before-shaking-and-introducing himself" routine).

....

While the shopper was touring a model, another prospect walked in. "Do you have to help her?" the shopper asked. "Oh, no," replied the SA. "I got her money already."

....

The shopper had to wait four minutes before she was even acknowledged.

....

When the shopper entered the sales office, the SA was talking with construction people. She didn't introduce herself, ask for the prospect's name, or provide her name.

....

Upon entering the sales center in the model, the shopper-prospect had difficulty seeing because the lights were off. When he asked the SA if the model was open, she answered, "Sure. Take a look." After the shopper returned from his tour, he asked the SA a few questions, which she answered while still working on her computer. When the shopper asked for floor plans, the SA provided them but she made no attempt to do any type of sales presentation. As the shopper left, she thanked him for stopping by,

....

The SA told the prospects to walk through model and then meet her back in the sales office if they had any questions.

....

During a shop that lasted 19 minutes, the SA never told the prospects her name or the builder's name, and she didn't ask the prospects for their names.

....

I've watched hundreds of shops in which the SA's never asked for the shopper's name. More often they say something like "Where are you folks from?" or "Here's the master bedroom, folks," or even worse, "How are you guys doing?"

The right way is to ask for the prospect's name and use it at least twice during the sales process. This builds rapport and trust.

Be cautious, however, not to overuse the name because it comes across as manipulative and "sales-y."

If a name is challenging to pronounce, ask for help. If necessary, write the name out phonetically so you say it correctly. People will appreciate your care.

Here are some quotes extracted from videos that are good examples of greeting a prospect:

....

"Hi, welcome to ABC Community. By the way, I'm Sue and you are.....?"

....

"As we move along the tour, do you mind if I take some notes on what you're most interested in?"

....

TIP: It's become popular among sales agents to carry a clipboard or tablet (e.g., iPad) for taking notes while making presentations. This is a great way to show interest in your prospects and to remember the information they've shared with you. Add the shop report to your tablet as well to help you remember questions.

SERVE REFRESHMENTS TO RELAX PROSPECTS

The more comfortable your prospects are, the more information they'll give you, and the better your sales presentation can be.

Keep in mind that *your* script isn't *their* script. Prospects enter the sales center with their own scripts. Their minds are filled with concerns like:

> *"Is buying a home the right thing to do?"*
>
> *"What if I don't have the money for the down payment?"*
>
> *"Can we afford a new home?"*
>
> *"If we wait, will we get a better deal?"*

With all these thoughts spinning around, it's essential to get your prospects to slow down and relax. One of the best ways to make prospects feel comfortable is to offer them something to eat or drink.

Think of all the places that offer food or beverages to their customers. Take Costco, for example, which serves samples throughout their stores. Eating makes shoppers calm and comfortable. Consequently, they shop longer and buy more. Some upscale clothing stores offer drinks and cookies for the same reason.

When I worked in property management, I noticed that most apartment communities had an Otis Spunkmeyer cookie oven. Mmmm, those fresh-baked chocolate chip cookies smelled wonderful! Where is the bakery department in most grocery stores? It's near the front of the store where the aroma of fresh-baked bread will waft out and entice customers in. The sense of smell powerfully impacts our feelings and memories.

At a Parade of Homes event in Tampa in which I was a speaker, a small builder cooked a pot roast in his model's oven during the event. The aroma enticed prospects to walk in and relax. The timeshare industry uses this food secret, too. If you've ever taken a 90-minute tour, you can probably recall having a full belly by the time it was over.

Walt Disney World knows the power of making customers comfortable. It can get pretty hot waiting in line for the popular attraction "Pirates of the Caribbean." To help patrons relax and get in the mood for the upcoming ocean experience while waiting in line, misting machines emit cool salt water on them. As my good friend John Palumbo would say, "They're getting them 'primed' for the pump.'"

> **TIP:** When serving drinks, don't use Styrofoam or logo cups that prospects will feel free to take. Instead, buy some good china cups for serving coffee. Using china cups encourages prospects to settle in and stay awhile. The longer the conversation flows in the sales center, the more you can dig for information, and the better you can plan your presentation. Is your budget too tight for real china? Go to Tuesday Morning or Target and buy cups that look like china.

ASK PROSPECTS IF THEY'VE VISITED YOUR COMPANY'S WEBSITE

Savvy home builders invest hundreds of thousands of dollars in their company websites. They hire top-notch techies, graphic designers, copywriters, and SEO experts to assure their websites are engaging, interactive, educational, and informative. Why? Because they know that over 95% of prospects first look at a company's website before setting foot in their sales office.

These days, prospects are doing homework and research on the internet long before they make a buying decision. They use home builders' websites to reduce the number of options and eliminate choices from consideration. Prospects who make the effort to come to your office are more than just "tire-kickers." They already know a lot about your community, your floor plans, and your builder. They're making the trip because they've been enticed by something of interest.

I always scratch my head in wonder when I watch a video mystery shop and the sales person never asks prospects if they've been to the company's website. This should be one of the first questions the sales person asks. Actually, I consider this to be one of the most important questions to ask in new home sales.

Asking prospects if they've visited the website provides valuable information that enables you to personalize and fine tune your presentation. In a very real sense, those who've visited your company's website have already visited your company. When they walk into your office for the first time, they're really "coming back" for a second time. And we all know that we have a better chance of converting a "be back" into a buyer.

Why in the world would you not find out if your prospect has visited your company's website? You have nothing to lose, and everything to gain.

I'll end this chapter with portions of shopping reports on two SA's who handled the Approach/Introduction step of the sales process perfectly:

••••••••••

The SA did a nice job with her approach and introduction. She offered the prospect refreshments and welcomed him to ABC Community. She determined he had been to the website. She also asked him how much time he had to spend with her.

••••••••••

When the shopper walked in, the SA did a great job qualifying and determining his needs. She told him what to expect on the visit. She discovered his needs, matched a home to his needs, and suggested he buy a home if she found the perfect match. She was not scared to let him know that the option of buying a home on the first visit could happen, if they found a match. After the presentation, she asked for the sale....and then found out he was actually looking for two investment properties. So, she asked for two sales!

••••••••••

CHAPTER 3

Getting To Know You

When I walked in, I obviously startled the SA because he kind of jumped up and looked like I caught him by surprise. I joked with him about being a slow day because I must have caught him sleeping. He laughed it off and we did our introductions. He didn't ask me a single question about my interest in buying a home. As we started looking through the model home, I mentioned something about it being boring sitting in an empty house all day. He said that it is boring, and

continued

to pass the time, "I surf the internet for porn all day." Of course being on camera I didn't know how to react so I brushed off the comment as though I didn't hear it. The SA then said, "As a matter of fact, had you come in a few minutes earlier you would have caught me with my hand down my pants surfing my computer." He said it jokingly and in fun as if two friends were talking. It took me totally by surprise. I laughed only because I didn't know what else to do. Later, when looking at the master bedroom he showed me the master closet. I commented on how big it was. His response was "Big enough to hang at least a dozen dead hookers in."

Discovery gives you input to match the right home to the right person.

The Discovery questions are vital in understanding moving motivation, size of family, time frame, preferences, how long customers have been looking, what other builders they've looked at and liked, etc.

The Discovery process encompasses the following questions on the shopping report:

- Did the SA determine how much time the prospect had to spend on the visit?
- Did the SA determine the prospect's moving time frame?
- Did the SA determine the prospect's preferences in a layout?
- Did the SA determine the prospect's price range?
- Did the SA determine the prospect's family size?
- Did the SA determine if the prospect is renting or has a home to sell?
- Did the SA determine how the prospect heard of the community?
- Did the SA determine how long the prospect has been looking?
- Did the SA determine the prospect's moving motivation?
- Did the SA determine the prospect's line of work?

The goal of Discovery is to be a true new home sales *counselor* and ask questions to understand the customer's situation, wants, and needs.

According to the dictionary, the definition of "counselor" is "a person who gives advice."

My best friend Ruth is a mental health therapist, a counselor. Ruth doesn't have clients walk in her office and within two seconds, she gives them advice. She spends many in-depth sessions asking introspective questions to understand their issues. Only when she has clarity does she recommend a course of action.

Interestingly, the same methodology utilized by a mental health counselor applies to onsite salespeople. Once you know the customer's issues, problems, challenges, and so forth, you can recommend a home that fits. Although this probably sounds extremely simplistic, I have found it not to be the case in the field. In my 27 years evaluating salespeople, it's apparent that the majority feel comfortable with a *product driven presentation* rather than a *prospect driven presentation.*

Although a product driven presentation may be more common, it most definitely is **not** the best way to achieve a sale. In fact, it can be self defeating. Unfortunately, I've watched more shops than I care to count in which the SA hardly asks anything. If questions were asked, they were usually the two standard ones: 1) "Is this your first visit?" and 2) "What's your price range?"

Here are some other examples of what **not** to do in the Discovery phase:

· · · · · · · · · · ·

The video showed the SA didn't ask anything. The shopper asked to see the model, and while the SA finished her lunch at her desk she pointed in the direction of the model and asked the shopper to go ahead and take a look. When the shopper returned, the SA asked,

"Do you have any questions?" It was less than a 10 minute tour and the shopper led himself, alone.

. . . .

SA didn't determine why the shopper was moving and who would be moving in the home. SA didn't narrow down what the shopper was looking for in terms of bed/bath/square feet. This would have helped her determine which floor plans to show. SA didn't determine price range.

. . . .

SA took a cell phone call. She didn't ask price range, traffic source, or how long the shopper had to visit.

. . . .

The shopper was asked what size home he wanted, how many bedrooms, and the price point. Then the SA showed an available home that was nothing like what the shopper said he wanted.

. . . .

Take a look at the time codes on one shop:

> *11:59 "How many people?"*
>
> *14:09 "Where do you live now?"*
>
> *15:58 "What's your timing?"*
>
> *19:34 "Are you familiar with the area?"*
>
> *23:17 "Are you a Floridian?"*
>
> *29:21 "Have you sold your house?"*
>
> *39:57 "What are your hobbies?"*
>
> *44:48 "What do you do?"*

While these are all valuable questions, they were asked far too late in the presentation. Think about it, at 39 minutes, 57 seconds, the shopper inquired about the customer's hobbies. Not only was this late in the presentation, but it turned out to be five minutes before it ended. Why is this important? Say, for example, the customer plays tennis. Perhaps there's a nearby park with free tennis courts. This is a great selling point. Or perhaps the customer does crafts and needs a separate room to work. It could have been a perfect cue for the SA to say something like, "This fourth bedroom would be ideal for crafts work, and look at the gorgeous view you'll enjoy."

Further, at 44 minutes, 48 seconds the customer was asked what type of work they do. This is priority information that needs to be gathered up front. Not only their line of work, but also further inquiry regarding the customer's need for a home office, travel, commuting, discussing their career, etc., is important. All of these kernels of information help you match the right home to the right person...and get the sale.

A strong, comprehensive shop averages 60 minutes. This one ended at 45:07.

The key is to dig deeper. When you're qualifying a prospect, standard Discovery questions are:

- What price range are you looking to stay within?
- Have you talked to a lender?
- When are you planning to move?
- How much money do you plan to put down on the home?

My friend and fellow sales trainer Jeff Shore focuses his sales training on Discovery and the question behind the question. He stresses discovering the customer's current dissatisfaction and then offering a future promise that benefits the customer.

The sales experience has slightly improved from years past when salespeople would do a "seven minute shop." The old routine went like this: The salesperson greets the shopper, points to the models (most had a trap system with fencing to wind customers back to the sales center), asks if they have any questions, hands them a brochure, and thanks them for visiting the models. We've come a long way baby but to truly be a *counselor*, it's imperative to **master** the Discovery part of the sales process.

How?

While the Discovery questions mentioned previously are good questions, they're not the best questions to help you get the sale. No matter how your prospect answers them, you're still not obtaining enough information to get a full picture in order to create an effective close.

I always encourage SA's to find out what their prospects do for a living. This is a great non-threatening way for you to get an indication of how much money the prospect makes per year. More importantly, it's an excellent opportunity for you to dig deeper, develop rapport, and gather valuable information without coming across as too "sales-y."

> **TIP:** In the Discovery process, take time to carefully and cautiously dig a little deeper with each question you ask. You'll be surprised how easily people will open up to you when they feel you're genuinely interested in them.

For example, I had a meeting with a financial planner and I was interviewing him to see if he and I would be a good business fit. One of the first things he asked me was "What do you do for a living?" I told him that I owned my own mystery shopping company and that I was also a speaker. I was ready for what I thought his next question was going to be, "How much money do you make per year?" but was pleasantly surprised when he said "Tell me how you got started in that business." For the next 20 minutes or so, I gave him a brief account of how and why I started Melinda Brody and Company. Before I realized it, he and I were talking like old friends! You see, when he turned the question around and started to show genuine interest in me and what I did for a living, I naturally relaxed. This is exactly what needs to happen in your Discovery process.

When you ask Discovery questions, be sure that they are indeed questions...not interrogations! People are usually very protective about sharing financial information with someone they've just met, so this area needs to be handled somewhat creatively. Discovering more about who your client is is far more useful in making the sale than just asking what they want their monthly payments to be.

Also, before asking any questions, you need to give the customer a reason *why* you want to ask, such as, "I don't want to waste your time today, so if you can help me with a few questions, I'll be able to point you in the right direction today. Is this okay with you?"

> **TIP:** Use a clipboard, tablet, or something to take notes on your tour. Nothing screams "I'm important" more than writing down what your customer is saying is important.

The next important point is to *remember* what they told you. Write it down. I know you know this, but we don't always do what we know we should. If we did, we wouldn't have to lose 20 pounds or go 80 mph on the highway when the speed limit is 65 mph or let the clutter build up in our homes!

Here are actual strong quotes taken from effective Discovery we videoed:

....

"What's important to you in your new home?"

....

"My role is to match your needs with a floor plan."

....

The SA asked many great qualifying questions and was able to determine the shopper's current situation, moving motivation, and time frame. SA asked the shopper what her "must haves" were in a new home.

....

> **TIP:** Find out what the customer's "must haves" and "can they live without it" are. A true sales "counselor" is a matchmaker. Your matchmaker formula is **"Customers' Needs + Customers' Price Range = Floor Plan You Show."** It's a winning match — and a sale!

CHAPTER 4

Who Cares About The Clubhouse?

My husband asked the SA what the community had to offer. The SA, while seated on the couch, threw his arms back and said "ABSOLUTELY NOTHING." He did zero to sell the community. Instead, he told us about another ABC builder community and emphasized how much better that community was. He said the homes were $20,000 cheaper there for the same models.

SELLING THE COMMUNITY PROPERLY IS THE DIFFERENCE BETWEEN LANDING A SALE AND $0

Selling the Community is comprised of discussion with the customer on lifestyle, surrounding area, and amenities. The goal is to deliver a customized, personalized community presentation that reflects what the prospective buyer says is important (*not* what you think is important).

It may be wonderful that a community is on an award-winning golf course with a million-dollar wow clubhouse that overlooks a state park. But if I'm not a golfer nor much of a socializer, none these features are important to me. I may be the customer who travels and when I'm home I'm a homebody. If that's the case, to me, frankly, all your amenities are wasteful and the homeowner's association fees are too high!

To sell the community correctly, you must first gauge customer interest with introspective questions. Based on the responses, you'll know what to emphasize or de-emphasize in your sales presentation.

As I cover Selling the Community, it will be helpful for you to keep in mind the following questions on the shopping report:

- Did the SA determine the prospect's knowledge of the area?
- Did the SA offer information regarding schools?
- Did the SA offer information on shopping?

- Did the SA offer information on surrounding areas and/or highways?
- Did the SA use visual aids to enhance the presentation?
- Did the SA discuss the community's amenities, if applicable?
- Did the SA offer information on HOA, CDD, or club membership fees, if applicable?
- Did the SA discuss the overview of community (# of homes, layout, etc.), if applicable?
- Did the SA trial close on the community?

Our video shops provide numerous examples of SA's incorrectly Selling the Community:

···········

"Here are all the floor plans and all the premiums on the lots."

···········

"This area is divided into three phases, blah, blah, blah...."

···········

The SA's working at ABC Development are selling lifestyle and golf course living, yet neither one took advantage of the fact that they could use a golf cart to tour the community. This screams lifestyle and country club living....need to learn to take advantage of those perks.... Especially when you have a lot of prospects from New York, etc....and cruising around the community in November on a golf cart is a big deal."

···········

There are some things you absolutely should never say about a community. Additionally, there's information you absolutely should know because the probability is high that you'll be asked.

> **TIP:** Keep the Selling the Community stage solely focused on meeting your customer's needs. It's inappropriate to make personal or any other type of negative commentary. Unless you're moving in with your customers, it doesn't matter what you think.

In one video shop, the SA said, *"I'm from the west coast. I moved here to follow a girl. This isn't my #1 place to live."*

Wrong, wrong, wrong.

The following was reported in another video shop:

Customer: *"Oh, that must be the new school,"* looking out the model window. *"What can you tell me about the teachers and the school?"*

SA: *"I don't know,"* emphasized with a shrug of the shoulders.

In 2012, Melinda Brody and Company evaluated over 1,200 onsite salespeople. When we studied customizing and personalizing the tour, a mere 38% did it. (I spoke about this topic at the 2013 Super Sales Rally at the International Builders Show.)

> **TIP:** Educate yourself on the school system in the vicinity of the community, from preschool to high school. This is an area of prime concern, as prospects with children often are targeting to reside in a specific school district.

FOUR MAGIC WORDS CAN DRAMATICALLY BOOST YOUR SALES

There are four magic words you must use throughout your community tour in order to be highly successful in sales. If I tell you what they are will you use them? Probably not, unless there's a financial incentive attached. Right? Okay, what if I tell you that these four magic words, when used properly, will instantly increase your sales? Now I know I have your attention!

The four words that will increase your sales performance every time are..... (drum roll please)......**What's important to you?**

In many of the video mystery shops that I review, I notice that sales people have an overwhelming urge to tell their new home prospects *everything* they can possibly think of about the home, the community, the warranty, the construction process, the energy efficiency, the builder's story, and on and on and on. While all of the information is valuable, it's more important to remember that too much information, or "feature dumping" as I call it, can greatly overwhelm prospects.

I suggest that before you introduce the community, builder, models or anything else, use the four magic words as your "transitional phrase." For example, before viewing the model home, ask your prospects:

- **What's important to you** in a new home?

Not only will this question get the dialogue rolling, it will steer personalization of your sales presentation to meet your prospect's specific needs.

Other key times to use the four magic words are:

- **What's important to you** in a new home builder?
- **What's important to you** in a home site?
- **What's important to you** in your new home community?

Each time you ask your prospect one of these questions, they'll be revealing their needs, wants, and desires in a new home. If a prospect tells you that energy efficiency is **important**, then make it a major talking point in your presentation. If they tell you that a good home warranty is **important**, break out the warranty manual and go to town discussing the value and merits of your builder's warranty program.

> **TIP:** Craft your presentation based on the customer's answer to the four magic words **"What's important to you?"** If you think something is important but your customer doesn't, then it's not important. The intent is to reveal their hot buttons and sell directly to those hot buttons.

The trick in doing the magic successfully is making sure that you're talking to your prospects about things that matter to them. Instead of trying to overload your prospects with everything under the sun about the home, you'll be able to create a highly targeted and effective presentation. Trust me when I tell you that your job will become much easier when you start asking them **"What's important to you?"**

Another important point to remember in your presentation is the "trial close." The trial close is a way of taking the prospect's temperature to gauge where they are in the likeability spectrum as well as the decision-making process. Some examples are:

"Does this look like a community that would work for you and your family?"

"Is this a community that would fit your lifestyle?"

"Can you picture yourself living here?"
"Of the communities you've visited so far, how do we compare?"

Here are some examples of Selling the Community correctly:
....

SA discussed the community and the surrounding area. She said the community was "in the heart of everything." SA offered to give the prospect a golf weekend package. She determined what he liked to do for fun. SA trial closed on the community.

....

SA is continually asking questions, taking the prospects temperature, checking in with her. "How does this work for you?"; "What do you think of this plan?"; "Is this enough room?"; "How does this compare?"; "Does this seem like a room that would suit your needs?"

....

SA did a great job selling the community after finding out what the customer was interested in. He showed the community overview using his marketing materials. He discussed the marina, security system, shopping, lagoons, etc. He painted a picture of the lifestyle that the community offers.

....

CHAPTER 5

We Are A Quality Builder (Snooze)

> The SA mentioned that her builder was "one of the best in the area, except for the illegal stuff that happened at corporate a few years back."

Selling the Builder is your opportunity to distinguish the builder you represent from your competition by engaging a compelling builder story. What gives you an edge? What makes you different and better than the others?

This stage of the sales process is easier than you may think. Just fill in the blank: "We are the only builder in [your city] who [your uniqueness]. Answers may range from "offers a no down payment plan" to "builds with brick" to "offers award winning energy features." Stack the deck to stand out from the crowd.

BUILDER'S STORY SEPARATES YOUR BUILDER FROM THE PACK

The goal of the builder story is to highlight the builder's uniqueness. The builder story also serves to build confidence with your customers, assuring them that your builder is trustworthy, solvent, and here to stay.

As I cover the Selling the Builder section, it will be helpful for you to keep in mind the following questions on the shopping report:

- Did the SA tell the builder's story?
- Did the SA point out the builder's uniqueness over the competition?
- Did the SA offer information on the warranty?
- Did the SA discuss the quality of construction?
- Did the SA build value of the product?

What makes one new home builder better than another new home builder? You may be thinking, "Really, aren't they all about the same?" True, they may use the same types of building materials, offer new homes in similar price ranges at a similar square footage, and have some type of warranty or guarantee to back up their product. But, the builder's story is the difference. It's your **secret sales weapon.** Your builder is your brand. The fact is, not all new home builders are created equal.

Here's a good example, based in another industry, one of my favorites – food: When you need to go to the grocery store, how do you select which store you'll shop in? After all, most grocery stores offer similar selections of canned foods, produce, meats, and other products. Right? Wrong? My guess is that you select a specific grocery store because of its "brand." You *trust* the brand. You *like* the brand. You're *loyal* to the brand. There's a reason Publix is the dominating grocery store throughout Florida and its market share is ever-increasing while Winn Dixie is closing stores quicker than you can say their slogan "The Beef People." It's all about the *brand* and *what that brand represents to consumers.*

By Selling the Builder, you not only gain credibility and trust with your prospects, but you're able to affiliate yourself with a brand that is much bigger than you are alone. As easy as it sounds, I wonder why sales people have a difficult time selling their builder. My guess is SA's don't really know how to sell the builder properly without sounding like they're reciting a speech memorized for ninth-grade graduation. Your builder's story needs to come naturally and not in the form of a Shakespearean soliloquy.

SELLING THE BUILDER POINTERS

The following suggestions will help you devise your builder's story:

- Always ask prospects **"What's important to you in a new home builder?"** (Remember the earlier lesson, ask "What's important to you?" Here it is again.) This takes pressure off of you and allows you to acquire valuable information from your buyer. Once you have answers, you can build your builder's story (no pun intended) to address these items. If, for example, "quality construction" is a hot button, adapt your presentation to include information about why and how *your* builder offers the best quality construction in town.

- Use the pronoun **"we"** when talking about your builder. Selling isn't an "us vs. them" scenario. I can't tell you how many times in video shops I hear new home sales people say to a customer: "Well, I can always ask **them** if that change can be made." You're on the same team as your builder. Use "we" to your advantage, such as "We offer an incredible value for this particular home...."

- **Do your homework—know your builder's story!** Know who the key players are (by name) in your company, when the business started, the number of homes sold annually, the number of communities they build in, and what sets your builder apart from the rest. Know your builder's USP (Unique Selling Proposition). If you need help with any this information, contact your builder's marketing or sales manager.

- **SA's, practice Selling the Builder by doing role playing with other sales team members. Sales Managers, make practice a focus of sales meetings.** The more comfortable you are in your delivery, the better you'll be in your sales presentation.

It's widely known in sales that in order to be *highly* successful, you've got to *believe in* the product or service you're selling. In new home sales, that product is your builder. You need to be 100% passionate about the builder you work for and the product they deliver.

Here are some things **not** to say or do when discussing your builder with a prospect:

....

"We are a family builder."

....

"We are a quality builder."

....

"There are older homes in the older community from the previous builders, but don't worry, they aren't slums."

....

47

TIP: A "family builder" and a "quality builder" are worn out , empty, and meaningless terms. Develop a compelling builder story, with details, that makes you stand out in the marketplace.

The sales person was pointing out the upgrades and features in the model home and the prospect asked why there were so many designer features in the model.

....

The sales person responded "The builder does this to get you to buy more upgrades."

....

"We have a great warranty....it covers everything bumper to bumper."

....

TIP: In his book *"To Sell Is Human,"* author Daniel Pink describes used car salesmen as having the most negative image according to a survey about salespeople. Therefore, it's wise not to make comparisons by mentioning a term used in car sales to describe your warranty

Also, when Selling the Builder, refrain from making statements against the competition. One SA made the flippant comment about a competitor who's known for stripping the land before building, "*ABC Builder never met a tree it didn't like.*"

In most cases, when a prospect enters the sales office, it's usually not the first or last stop they'll be making that day. They likely have scheduled visits to several new home communities, which they plan to do before making a purchasing decision. It could be highly detrimental to your success if you make a negative comment about the former builder they visited or the next one they're headed to.

Now, let me delve a little deeper into the advantage of Selling the Builder. As mentioned earlier, when a prospect enters *your* sales office, chances are they've been to your website and have seen something that piqued their interest enough to get them to physically come in person. It could be a specific floor plan, a price point, or even your community's amenity center.

Your job is to find out what attracted the prospect to your community. (As stated earlier, ask every prospect "Have you visited our website?") Let's say you've determined the prospect was on the website and they **love** the location of your community, the amenities that are offered, and the Wellington floor plan. You're thinking "slam dunk." Then, just as you go in for the "close," the prospect mentions that while they do indeed love your community, they have plans to visit several more before making a decision. Major bummer! Next, you say your goodbyes, promise to follow up, and watch them drive off into the sunset **knowing** that you'll probably never see them again.

> **TIP:** Never denigrate the competition. You gain nothing in terms of making the sale. The opposite happens, it makes you look desperate and unprofessional. If you do a good job Selling the Builder you represent, there's no need to make snide remarks about other builders.

Hmmmm, something is out of kilter. What could you have done to change this off-into-the-sunset scenario? Here are some easy tips to help you apply Selling the Builder, conquer the competition (nicely), and get the sale:

- Know **everything** about your competition. This includes pricing, floor plans, incentives, amenities, schools, and anything else that would be considered when making a purchase decision. Selling the Builder is just as much about selling the builder you represent as it is about being knowledgeable on who you're competing against.

- Create a notebook with **all** of your competitor's marketing collaterals. This way you can factually **show** the prospect **why** your Wellington floor plan is a better fit for them than the competition's Buttonwood. This allows you to make honest side-by-side comparisons without speaking negatively about another builder.

- Ask your prospects **what** other communities they're considering and **why**. This helps identify the customer's "hot buttons" and lets you take the sales process to the next level by clearly positioning yourself against the competition. Again, knowledge about competitors is essential. You can actually zoom in on a particular hot button and emphasize how well you fulfill their need, want, or desire. This strategy helps make the buyer realize that your new home is the best choice.

- **Set up** a firm follow-up appointment with your prospects. Encourage them to come back to see you after they've finished looking at the other communities because you're so positive that what you offer meets their specific needs. Ramp up your sales arsenal for this opportunity in order to make the grand finale impact and secure the sale.

- Throughout the sales process, as tempting as it may be, never, ever speak negatively about your competition. Instead **position** your builder and community as the leader in every aspect. Share enough information and the right information that leads your customer to make the buying decision with you.

Here are some excellent examples from video mystery shops of Selling the Builder:

············

SA said "We work with a national builder who has a separate display area for energy efficient items." Each item was explained in detail. The SA also engaged the shopper by showing him how great these features would be and how much money they would save on their power bill.

············

Great USP (Unique Selling Proposition) when discussing the builder. "We are the only builder in this area who uses R15 insulation...Mr. Williams, our CEO, pays your electric bill for one year!"

············

"You can knock on anyone's door and ask them how their experience was working with our builder. You'll be pleased with the answer."

············

CHAPTER 6

Walk This Way

> "I sometimes put a sign on the door that I'm out, but really I go to the mall shopping. You're not one of those secret shoppers, are you?"

Demonstrating the Home/Model is the highlight of the sales presentation, and it's where you focus on what interests the prospect. Avoid asking, "Would you like to have me join you in the model?" because they may say, "No, that's okay, we'll go look on our own." Take the lead with phrases like "Walk this way" and "Let's get started with the first model so I can point out the included features with our beautiful homes!"

The prospect needs a guide, and that person is you – guiding them all the way to a new home sales contract! Engage the prospect and allow them to fall in love with "their" home using the recommendations explained in this chapter.

Here are the questions from the "demonstration" section of our shopping report to keep in mind as you gain an understanding of Walk This Way:

- Did the SA show the prospect available floor plans?
- Did the SA demonstrate a model or available home?
- Did the SA talk in terms of benefits as well as features?
- Did the SA personalize the demonstration to the prospect's specific needs?
- Did the SA discuss exterior features (landscaping, elevations, etc.)?
- Did the SA trial close on the home?

PAINT A TRUE PICTURE OF "HOME" DURING THE TOUR

The goal of demonstrating the homes/models is to have the customer visualize themselves living in one of them. The sales agent who gives a personalized, customized tour is the one that makes sales.

The use of descriptive wording during the home/model demonstration will help you. Here's a perfect example with, what else, one of my other favorite subjects as you've noticed by now, food: We recently were at a local farmers market looking at some homemade cheesecake cupcakes. The vendor asked, "Do you guys like quality cheesecake?" We responded, "Of course." The vendor replied, "Well, these will make your eyes roll back in your head." We laughed, bought, ate, and looked skyward.

As mentioned in chapter 4, a benchmark study Melinda Brody and Company conducted in 2012 revealed that a mere 38% of SA's shopped used the "P and C" approach—"personalizing and customizing." It's difficult to personalize and customize the model tour if you haven't asked "What's important to you?" up front. You simply end up delivering a boring talking-head, feature-dumping presentation.

Here are some poor examples of Demonstrating the Home/Model:

· · · · · · · · · · ·

SA showed the prospect five models. The prospect was an elderly lady and they walked to all of them. He never offered her a drink. He spent more time in the basements of the homes than in the living space. He had the prospect selecting features and paint colors, yet never even trial closed her. He also told the shopper that "Lotsa older people live here."

···········

"This is our entry-level ranch. The rooms will be on the small side."

···········

"You can see our model is all dolled up but our standard features are still pretty nice."

···········

"We have the standard tub, standard tile, standard ledge, standard light, standard mirror, standard faucet, standard shower seat..."

···········

"I don't think you'll like the kitchen in that one, I don't like the kitchen in this one.....for me, the dining room opening to the kitchen is great. I shouldn't talk about myself."

···········

The prospect indicated that he'd seen and liked a certain floor plan on the builder's website. The SA said: "Yeah that one is a pretty popular seller, I'm not really sure why. Personally it's my least favorite." She then went on to explain (in full detail) why it was her least favorite.

···········

"I love the entrance of the home we're going into to..... I love everything about this house."

···········

"I can show you an inventory home. It's not decorated. Kind of like a woman without her makeup on."

TIP: What if your prospect hates the home you love? Your job is to help others find the home of their dreams. Keep your opinions to yourself.

....

The SA was sending her prospect to another one of the builder's communities in order to see a decorated model of a floor plan that she was interested in buying. She then said: "Be careful with Susan. She will try to talk you into buying from her in that community instead of here."

....

A perfect example of focusing on giving people what they want is a Heineken beer commercial a few years back during the Super Bowl. It showed the wife walking into her newly-designed

TIP: If you think another one of your builder's communities is more suitable for the prospect, take the customer there yourself or call the sales person at that community and set an appointment for the prospect.

clothes closet and all her girlfriends screaming with delight at the space for her collection of shoes. Simultaneously, the men walked into the husband's new closet and screamed when they saw it was a walk-in beer closet.

TAKE COMMAND BY STEERING THE CONVERSATION

My team watches countless SA's on video do their blah, blah, blah presentation and discuss every feature they offer ad nauseam. It's challenging to stay awake just watching them, so I can only imagine how the prospect feels.

Great SA's let the conversation "breathe." They pause. They're comfortable with some silence. They ask great involvement questions while touring the models, such as:

"Who's the cook in the family?"
"Do you have family visit often?"
"What would you use this room for?"
"Do you entertain often?"

When I was a shopper, I distinctly remember touring a model with a huge country-style kitchen. The SA went on and on demonstrating the kitchen, its spaciousness, the expansive counter space, cabinet space, large enough for an eight-seat table, etc. The more he demonstrated, the more turned off I became. All I saw was a huge room that I would hardly use and it would be one more thing for me to have to keep clean. (Hey, am I the only one who hides birthday presents in the oven? As my mom would answer to "What's for dinner?"..."Reservations!") The SA assumed my hot buttons but never once asked. Consequently, he was completely off base in his assumptions.

KEEP YOUR PROSPECT FOCUSED BY DRAWING ATTENTION TO ONE FEATURE

The demonstration is also the prime time for you to help focus your prospect on one selection that meets a key need they've expressed. I always say, "Your prospect has ADD and you're the Ritalin!" Most people are unable to retain multiple items simultaneously.

At one community I shopped, the SA asked me how many bedrooms and baths I wanted. When I replied three bedrooms, two baths, he said, "We have 38 different plans that are three bedrooms." The more choices you offer your prospects, the more confused they become.

A great example of limiting the focus to one selection is Costco's way of selling. They limit choices. When I go to buy my favorite 0% Greek yogurt, they have two brands, Fagé and Kirkland. In contrast, when I go to Publix to buy yogurt, there's an entire shelf of choices, dozens of brands, types, flavors, etc. I get dizzy looking at the display and it's hard to make a decision.

> **TIP:** Focusing your demonstration on one (or two) special features is far more effective than trying to present the entire list to a prospect. Limit the choices and you'll increase your sales!

Here are some great examples of Demonstrating the Home/Model:

∙∙∙∙∙∙∙∙∙∙∙

Throughout the model tour, the SA continues to check-in with the shopper "Would this work? How does this feel? Would this room be a good office space? How do you feel about the open floor plan?"

∙∙∙∙∙∙∙∙∙∙∙

The SA was very thorough in her demonstration. She determined the floor plans that would fit the prospect's needs. She personalized the presentation by asking about his furniture and confirmed that the size would work. SA trial closed.

....

SA had excellent product knowledge. Prospect asked about several options and she had the pricing at her fingertips.

....

Two SA's were observed on video giving the key to the prospect to open the door to the model as if they were unlocking the door to their new home.

....

CHAPTER 7

Demo The Dirt

> "The builder builds their inventory homes on the worst lots because people in a hurry will buy them anyway."

Demonstrating the Home Site/Location is often overlooked by SA's, maybe because it's a part of the sales process that can be quite a tough challenge. If there's an available home ready that's a plus, but often you have to "Demo The Dirt," and that takes some creativity. The goal of Demonstrating the Home Site/ Location is to find out what's important to your prospects in a home site and then **physically** visit the site and connect the dots, so to speak.

63

Here are the questions on demonstrating a home site/location from our shopping report:

- Did the SA use the site map to show available locations, if applicable?
- Did the SA tour the locations with the prospect, if applicable?
- Did the SA use benefit selling for the location, if applicable?
- Did the SA trial close on the location, if applicable

THERE'S PLENTY YOU CAN SAY ABOUT A HOME SITE

Demonstrating a beautifully merchandised model or gorgeous state-of-the-art clubhouse is relatively easy but the home site is a bit more challenging because it's just an empty lot.

Here are some things **not** to say:

···········

"We have lots of lots."

···········

When the prospect objected to the view of a trailer park behind the lots, he shrugged and said, "It's South Carolina."

···········

"Let's take your car...mine has dog hair all over the seats."

···········

"I'm kinda in a jacked-up truck, so do you want to follow me?"

....

"As we drive over to the lots, please excuse the crap in my car."

....

> **TIP:** Even if you're in a double wide and just opened, telling your prospect "there are plenty of lots available" is the worst thing to say. The right way is for you to identify the plan and discuss with your prospect what they would like to view. Then, narrow down the choices and show only two locations.

How do you take a barren, boring empty lot and transform it into a super, sexy potential home site to your prospects? The answer is simple: **visualization.** Visualization means getting your prospects to "see" themselves living on that home site. How do you do this? Here are some ideas:

- **Use the phrase "home site" instead of lot.** This is a small but significant step in helping your prospects visualize. Which would you rather live on, a "lot" or a "home site"?
- **Physically take your prospect to the home site.** You're doing yourself and your prospect a major disservice if you don't

> **TIP:** Your car is your mobile office. Always keep it clean, washed, detailed, and ready to drive prospects to the select home sites.

physically walk the home site. Most people can't visualize what a new home looks like from viewing only a floor plan. The same is true with the home site. Also, by setting foot on the home site, you're establishing a sense of ownership that can't be garnered looking at a site map.

- **Ask your prospect questions about what they like to do outside.** Engaging your prospects on how they would use the outdoor space allows you to segue into the actual experience of living there. Once you find out what they like to do outdoors, you can paint the picture for them in detail. If they enjoy gardening, point out an area that would be excellent for planting. If they have children, demonstrate how the yard space could accommodate a back yard jungle gym or swing set. Also, point out the obvious, i.e., the beautiful trees or the spacious back yard.

- **Trial close the prospect on the home site.** You want your prospects to "fall in love" with the home site the same way they fall in love with the home. Trial close with, "Isn't this home site the perfect location? Look at the gorgeous greenbelt you have behind the home..."

It's all about visualization and painting that ideal experience for your prospects.

Here are some excellent examples of visualization:

....

The SA drove her prospect to the home site. Instead of just pointing it out, she said: "You can't appreciate the view from the street." Together they walked the entire home site and the SA asked the prospect how he would use the area. She asked many questions and discovered he was an avid golfer. She emphasized how this particular home site offered the best of both worlds: a golf course view with a retention pond as well. When she finished, she trial

> **TIP:** While you're physically standing in the prospect's potential new back yard, take them to the good times ahead. For example, "Can you 'see' yourselves enjoying a glass of wine after work while sitting in this back yard watching your children running and playing with Fluffy as the sun quietly sets behind the canopy of trees?"

closed by asking him if he would enjoy living on "his" new golf course home site.

....

The SA showed the home site and how it would be private with a beautiful view of the woods.

....

It was a premium corner home site and the SA pointed out how it would accommodate a large pool and covered patio area so his family could really "live the Florida outdoor life."

....

CHAPTER 8

You Can't Handle
The Truth (Or Objections)

> The prospect objected to the sound from the
> highway being loud. The SA responded, "It's not loud.
> I don't hear anything."

Objections can be "deal breakers" if they're not identified and overcome. The goal of handling objections (which may very well be truthful) is to flush them out early in the conversation and respond in a calm, convincing way that neutralizes the prospect's concerns.

These are the questions on handling objections from our shopping report:

- Did the SA use empathy regarding the objection?
- Did the SA clarify the prospect's concerns through questioning?
- Did the SA offer solutions and/or suggestions to overcome the objection?
- Did the SA make sure the prospect was satisfied with the solution?

SUCCESSFULLY OVERCOME OBJECTIONS BY TURNING THEM INTO SELLING POINTS

Objections can make you nervous and flustered unless you're prepared with ready responses. These four tips will help you handle objections with finesse and flip them to work toward making the sale: 1) Empathize with the objection to validate the prospect, show empathy, and let them know you heard the objection; 2) Ask deeper questions to determine *why* it's an objection *and how big* of an objection it is; 3) Offer solutions or recommendations to overcome the objection, if applicable; 4) Confirm with the prospect that the objection is resolved.

Here are some poor examples of handling objections:

··········

The prospect expressed concern over selling her home. This was not addressed.

··········

The prospect expressed concern over the size of one of the secondary bedrooms. The SA explained that the sizes were different in other floor plans. The SA did not question deeper to determine why this was a concern. The SA did not confirm that she had overcome the objection.

··········

Prospect mentioned that he didn't like walking through the bathroom in the master to get to the closet. The SA said: "That's how they're building homes today."

··········

Prospect objected to the washer/dryer being on the second floor. She was concerned about flooding. The SA explained why this was not a concern, stating "'Many people from the north are accustomed to having basements for their washer/dryers. Having a washer/dryer on the second floor is something they're not accustomed to."

··········

The prospect was concerned about needing hurricane shutters. The SA told her that was not a concern in Central Florida. SA did not show empathy or ask questions to clarify or confirm that she had overcome the objection.

··········

> **TIP:** Empathy goes a long way in handling objections. "I understand your concern" is validating the concern rather than going directly into an answer. Always show empathy when a prospect has an objection. It assures prospects you're listening and that their input and comments are valuable.

Here are some common objections and how to neutralize them:

Objection: The lots are too small.

Solution: When I conduct sales seminars, a common objection brought up by the sales team is "The lots are too small." Here's how to counter the concern: Put on your prospect shoes for a moment and pretend you just drove into your community. Are you looking at the homes? Are you noticing the space between the homes? If you seriously thought the homes were too close, why would you continue to drive to the sales center? The answer is, you wouldn't! So, the "lots are too small" is merely an observation, not a deal breaker.

I live in a small home (less to clean! yeah!) on a cul-de-sac. The homes are close together. I find this to be a *plus* because I see and talk with my neighbors when they're taking out the garbage or mowing their lawn. I know all six neighboring families – kids' and dogs' names included! In contrast, friends of mine who have bigger homes on larger home sites say they don't know the neighbors on either side of them because they never see them.

Objection: There's not enough space in the kitchen.

Solution: Again, always begin with "I understand" or "That's a good point," and then transition into "Tell me about your current kitchen." Next, show the prospect creative ideas on how to maximize space, i.e. stacked containers and store appliances they don't use on a daily basis. Additionally, mention how quick and easy a smaller kitchen is to clean.

Objection: The homes are too expensive.

Solution: Prospects want to get the most for their money.

TIP: Never assume a prospect's comment that sounds like an objection is a deal breaker. After saying "I understand your concern about the size of the kitchen" continue with "Tell me more about that..." This information gives you more concrete details about the issue so that you can directly deal with and resolve it.

Your "I understand" and "Tell me more about that" may reveal that they're discussing pricing on a competitor's home. You need to do a price comparison to what they've seen. Of course, not all homes are created the same and it boils down to what's most important in their new home. Some builders have an empty home and customize with options while others "include everything."

Additionally, you can lead the conversation in terms of monthly investment rather than overall price. This is a point in which most prospects have no idea what the payment is on a $250,000 home with 20% down on a 30-year fixed-rate mortgage of 4%. If you can work up a good faith estimate, you can show the breakdown. If the monthly investment is higher than a competitor's, you can "reduce to ridiculous" and simply say "For only $10 more a day, you can own this home that has all the features you want, the golf course view, the granite countertops, the gorgeous stone fireplace, etc."

TIP: The bottom line is building value. Otherwise, price is always going to be the objection. If the prospect wants it, price is no longer an objection. Your job is to make them want it!

Now, here are some excellent demonstration examples from mystery shops...

··········

*The prospect was objecting about the size of the pantry in the kitchen. She wondered aloud why the builder would have made the pantry so small, and said it was not very efficient. Instead of getting defensive, the SA immediately **thanked** the prospect for her feedback. She then went on to say that the builder always appreciates getting input from buyers. They then discussed options for a larger pantry that would accommodate the buyer's needs.*

··········

The prospect objected to the community being too far out. The SA responded with, "I understand. Tell me more about that." The prospect went on to mention the lack of conveniences nearby. The SA said that is just the reason other buyers love the community. The relaxing, country feel overrode the extra few minutes to drive to the grocery store. She checked in with the prospect and whether she agreed, and the prospect said she hadn't thought of it that way, mirroring back. "It was nice to be 'out in the country' a bit."

··········

CHAPTER 9

Let's Wrap Things Up

> "If you thought this was long (referring to the feature list), wait until you see the F........ING contract!" (Yes, he dropped the F-bomb).

Closing is all about timing. There are signals. If you miss them, you miss the window of opportunity to take the sale to the next level.

The goal of closing is to wrap things up with a win-win. Your customers commit to a gorgeous, brand new home that fits their needs and that they can afford. You're the reason they're improving their lives by asking them to move to the next step: sign the contract.

Here are the closing questions from our shopping report:

- Did the SA create a sense of urgency?
- Did the SA review a wish list and discuss pricing with the prospect?
- Did the SA fully explain the purchase procedure?
- Did the SA determine if the prospect has spoken to a lender(s)?
- Did the SA offer information on the preferred lender(s)?
- Did the SA determine when the prospect would be making a buying decision?
- Did the SA proactively suggest moving forward?
- Did the SA discover the customer's concern with buying today?
- Did the SA ask directly for a firm future appointment?

SEIZE THE WINDOW OF OPPORTUNITY OR YOU'LL LOSE THE SALE

I can best explain the "window of opportunity" with you by recalling two incredible events.

Jerry Seinfeld was coming to the Bob Carr Auditorium in Orlando about five years ago. I stood in line for four hours to get great tickets. I was successful, landing terrific front-row seats for my boyfriend Howard and me and my best friend Ruth and her husband.

I'm a **huge** Seinfeld fan.

I set my mind on two goals for the night of the show: 1) talk to Jerry Seinfeld; and 2) get him to sign my Seinfeld DVD set, seasons 1 & 2.

We went, and at the end of the show, Jerry did questions-and-answers with the audience.

No time to be shy. The window opened. I had to go for it. I needed a strategy because people were screaming out questions: "How's Superman?" "Are you coming back to TV?" I had to think fast. What would catch his attention? How could I personalize my question?

I know. I'll shout a question about his wife. "How's Jessica's cookbook doing?" I yelled.

He responded! I was talking to Jerry Seinfeld! Checkmark on goal number one!

Next was the DVD autograph.

We were at the 8 p.m. show, and Jerry was also doing a 10 p.m. gig.

I told my friends that we were going to hang around and wait for Jerry to exit the building. They laughed and left. My boyfriend Howard was "in."

We waited and waited. About 20 people were outside in a light rain. Luckily we had umbrellas. I was on a mission. The security guard stuck his head out to announce, "Jerry is not signing anything. He's in a hurry. He has to immediately getting into his town car and fly out."

I thought, "Good way to thin the line." 15 people departed. Howard wanted to leave. "Ye of little faith," I thought.

I knew the guard had made the "He's got to get out of here fast" announcement to shrink the line. (Being from New York does have its privileges.)

Sure enough, at the end of the 10 p.m. show, the guard stuck his head out and said, "No pictures, just line up."

I got my Jerry Seinfeld autograph on my DVD set! I successfully seized my window of opportunity! Check mark on goal number two!

In new home sales, the closing window is there. You just need to go for it before the window shuts.

Another example of grabbing the window of opportunity when you have it is documented on YouTube. Singer/Piano Man Billy Joel was performing at Vanderbilt University. At the end of his concert, he opened the mike for questions and answers, and one brave student stood up and asked if he could play with Billy Joel right then and there. Billy graciously said "Okay" and they belted out an awesome "New York State of Mind." Talk about a closer!

Let's Wrap Things Up

Success can happen, you just have to ask. A closer is an asker. If you don't ask, the answer is always "no." If you do ask, wonderful rewards come to fruition.

Here are some ways **not** to close caught in our video shopping:

....

At one point, SA gives the price of the home, and says "But, honestly, we will take less for that. We're not supposed to do this, but I think if you offer $200K that would be a good offer. What do you think?"

....

SA mentioned she had "50 lots left."

....

Prospect asked, "How long would it take to build one of these?" (Huge buying signal) SA answered quickly and went on demonstrating. Very long and unfocused presentation showing way too many choices.

....

"If you have any questions, let me know."

....

"Call me when you want to come back out."

....

SA mentions mortgage person who can help with numbers. (like looking at a car and the sales representative can't tell you a payment)

....

"Would you like me to do a good faith estimate?"

> **TIP:** Open your window of opportunity by changing questions to a subtle request, such as "Let's go back to the office and I'll show you your monthly investment."

....

"I'm supposed to ask you three times for a check."

....

"You got my card, call me with any questions."

....

"Well, it's the end of the month and they (the builder) really need to make the numbers, so I'm sure I can get you a better price."

....

"Between you and me, we can just ignore those lot premiums."

....

"I didn't get your information but you have mine. Did I give you a price sheet?"

CREATE URGENCY TO MOTIVATE THE PROSPECT TO BUY — NOW!

Urgency, it still works after all these years. People want what others want.

Here's a perfect example: My boyfriend Howard and I are very different. I bought my car in 10 minutes online. He had been looking for 10 loooooooooooooong years for his dream car. But not just any car. A 1966 Royal Blue Pontiac GTO. It's been his screensaver. He had a photo of one in our bathroom. He would point out the cars as we drove around town. (I would get even by pointing out women's shoes I liked!)

One day, Howard got excited when he saw an ad online for just the car he was after and he asked me to come along to see it. When we drove up to the seller's house, I swear everything happened in slow motion. The garage door slowly opened, dry ice poured out, and when the smoke cleared, there it was...a 1966 Royal Blue Pontiac GTO.

Next, out came Joe, the seller; he looked exactly like actor Tony Danza. The conversation went like this:

"How yooze doin?" (strong New Yawk accent)

"Ok, where are you from in New York?" I asked.

"'Brooklyn."

I turned to Howard and said, "Okay, we're screwed." (In New York, everyone negotiates to the "nth" degree.)

Howard and I looked over the car. It was in mint condition. We looked under the hood, pretending to know what we were looking at. Even I got excited! It was perfect.

"Wanna test drive it?" asked Joe.

We did. It was noisy (which is by design) and Howard loved

it because I couldn't talk. Well, I could talk, but he couldn't hear me over the noise.

Back at Joe's house, Joe trial closed with, "Well, what do ya think?"

Howard hesitated.

Joe said, "I'll give yooze guys some space."

Howard asked me. I replied, "Buy the damn car! It's perfect. The price, color, condition, etc."

Howard said, "Hmmmm, I just can't make the decision so fast...I want to sleep on it, think about it...not sure...it's a lot of money."

He told Joe he was going to think it over, and we left.

The next day, Howard called me in a panic on my cell phone.

"Joe called and said he has another buyer interested who's coming back today at 4 p.m. What should I do?" I told him, **"Buy the damn car."**

Now, did Joe really have another buyer? I don't know, but it doesn't matter. The urgency pushed Howard off the fence and into Joe's hands. Joe got the sale.

How many of your prospects are sitting on the fence? How many want to "think about it," "sleep on it," "pray about it"?

The following are excellent examples of closing the sale:
....

SA did excellent trial closes throughout the presentation. She said:

'If we found your home today, would you be ready to move forward?"

....

SA asked for a deposit of $5000 to lock down home site #17. He created a sense of urgency on the home site.

....

SA gave many excellent trial closes throughout the tour, such as "What do you think of this house?"; "How would you rate this home on a scale of 1 to 10?"; "What do you think of this one?"; "Which home did you like best?"; "What kind of investment are you making for your down payment?"; "Would you be able to move forward if I got you a good price reduction on that?"

....

"If I can get you this, can we move forward? Can we do paperwork today?"

....

"Can you close by the end of the month?"

....

My theory is that many SA's are timid about the "closing" because it equates with being pushy and obnoxious, the type of salesperson who annoys you to death. You certainly don't want to be put in that category. Instead, you swing all the way to the tour guide category and just provide information, show a lovely model home, and hope and pray the prospects will grace you with a return visit.

Next story. Howard and I went to gorgeous Sedona, Arizona six years ago. We have an Orlando, Florida timeshare, and through RCI we traded our week for the Arizona location. Like Forest Gump says, "Life is a box of timeshares, I mean, chocolates, you never know what you're going to get." We were thrilled. The timeshare was great. When you check into a timeshare, what's the next thing they offer? A free gift. Free gift is code for "We want to upgrade you. All you have to do is take a 90 minute tour."

If you're ever in this situation, don't be fooled. Ninety minutes in time share language is actually a "three hour tour."; sing it, Gilligan Island-style if you are old enough to remember that TV show. What's the gift? A sunset tour of the Grand Canyon, taking the bus there and back, a half-day excursion. That sounded pretty good, and besides, I like to study and blog about salespeople. So we agreed to the "90 minute tour."

We arrived at the timeshare sales office on time and were escorted to a waiting area with four other couples of baby boomer age. We all looked like sitting ducks. I wondered if the sales team was peeking around the corner and sizing us up as we so often do with prospects at our model centers. I purposely "dressed down" and put on my WalMart look. After all, I am in for the gift. No upgrade necessary for the timeshare. Practice with me, Howard, just say "No!"

We were given juice, muffins, fruit, an entire spread. There were pictures on the wall of timeshare destinations around the world, and a Big Book on the table of happy timeshare owners and their locations. Sales trainer John Palumbo would call this "priming the pump," getting us "juiced" so to speak, a warm up for what's to come. All these purchasers can't be wrong, can they? We were in the waiting room about 15 minutes.

In walked Brad and he asked for us by name. He was about 30 years of age, very friendly and nice, and he escorted us to the Big Room. The Big Room had about 25 round tables, and each sales-person took a couple to a table. Again, more food. Hard to keep saying "no" when you're eating. Hey, wait, I know all this. It's what I do and teach to new home sales people. That's because it usually works. As I discussed earlier, food relaxes people. So does calming music. Relaxed people lower their guard and are more likely to take out their wallet.

Then, Brad made his move, stating "I bet the two of you came here today for the free gift and told each other to just say 'no' if asked to buy anything. Right?" Geez. Was he listening with a glass to our room? He hit the objection right up front, discussed the elephant in the room immediately.

"Oh, yeah," we sheepishly admit.

"Well, no worries," said Brad reassuringly. "We're going to discuss whether upgrading is even a good option for you and go from there." (Note: The takeaway close "This is not for everyone.")

The discovery process started. Brad took out his clipboard and proceeded to ask us questions with an assumptive closing agenda. The questions rolled out: "Where do you like to vacation? If you were to take two weeks of vacation this year, where would you go? Are you beach people or do you like the mountains?"

The inquiries continued for about 30 minutes. Of course, we were eating, relaxed, and the questions were conversational. I knew exactly what was happening. Brad was smoothly narrowing down our choices and getting us to engage. All good stuff.

As we continued to sit in the Big Room, Brad brought out the Big Book. I had warned Howard about the Big Book. Since Howard is a nice, homespun guy from Ohio and I can bring out my "Don't mess with me" New York persona, I warned Howard that if he touched the Big Book and start looking at the photos of all the timeshare choices, it was too engaging and the selling process would continue and be longer. My goal was to get the gift, be as nice as possible, and be out in 30 minutes. Clearly, I was losing.

Brad saw me shift in my seat when he took out the Big Book. I didn't reach for it, so Brad gave it to Howard and aimed his questions directly to him. Brad completely quit making eye contact with me.

Brad then ramped up his hard pitch about the upgrade, how we can will the timeshare to our children, etc. Five times. I counted. It was painful. We were squirming. Howard told Brad that we were not upgrading. But since he's a social worker, he said it *nicely*.

I was more direct and my New York persona came out, "We're not upgrading. We just came for the gift, and we need to move on." Brad said "Of course," and then asked if his manager could come over and ask our opinion for a survey. We agreed. I didn't see it coming. "Survey" is code for "takeover" or "TO."

The manager started asking us about upgrading. We continued with the "No!" He tried and tried for about 15 minutes. It was beyond annoying.

I piped up, "Brad, you did a TO." I explained what I do professionally and Brad proceeded to totally blow me off. I promised him I had no camera and wasn't mystery shopping him. It wasn't working. We were now at 105 minutes.

Brad asked Howard if he wanted to see the model. Pretty poor sales tactic. Over 90 minutes of qualifying, then he offered to show us something. Mr. Nice Guy Howard says, "Sure."

We went to look at the model, five minutes max. Brad attempted more rapport building. Then we returned to the Big Room. At last, the free gift was going to come out! Or so we thought. We sat for about 20 minutes waiting. This is now awful; I'm impatient *and* on vacation. The manager came over to Howard and me to tell us "Just a few more minutes."

Next, they hit us with the referral pitch. If we gave them five names of friends/family, they would give us a restaurant gift certificate. *Are you kidding?* I said to Howard, "Okay, let's give him the neighbors around our street that we don't like." At long last, the angels are singing now, the gold doors open, the chorus is singing, and out comes the lady with the gift certificate.

The rest of the story is that the sunset tour of the Grand Canyon turned out to be a bust. The timeshare gods above were punishing us. It was a white out. Snow everywhere. We couldn't see a thing. It was like going to a skyscraper roof-top restaurant in the fog.

Well, at least I got some good speech and book material.

"Closing" doesn't have to be pushy, annoying, or obnoxious like this timeshare story. If you do everything leading up to the close – build rapport, really listen, ask great questions, personalize the tour, and ask trial closing questions, you will have earned the right to wrap it up!

CHAPTER 10

Fantastic Follow Up Finale

Dear Chelsea,

I just want to thank you again for your interest in ABC Estates, and I want to extend to you my best wishes in your search for a new home. As you know, Best Builders has been in the business of creating new homes for over 55 years. We would love to make you part of our growing family.

You may, of course, reach me at anytime if you have questions, or if you would like to set an

continued

appointment to talk in more detail.

Thank you once again for your interest in Best Builders.

Sincerely,

Sally Salesperson

It's imperative to not only follow up with your prospects, but follow up in a customized, personalized manner that makes a lasting imprint. Remember, you've got a lot of competition out there, so your follow up needs to be fantastic.

In our shopping reports, many SA's receive points for doing the follow up but the follow up they send is bland and boring like the one above. It's better than not following up, but not by much. This example lacks personalization and personality. It seems like a template that could be sent to any prospect who visited. Also, notice, there's no "call to action." The problem with not including a call to action is it puts the return visit in the hands of the prospect.

Here are the follow up questions from our shopping report:

- Was follow up received by e-mail?
- Was follow up received by telephone?

- Was follow up clear and concise?
- Did the follow up proactively suggest moving forward in the sales process?

SILENCE MEANS NO SALES

Our typical scenario is we send our shoppers out as an "A" prospect. They're ready, willing, and able to buy. Their home is sold, they're the sole decision maker, they love what you're showing them, and they fill out your registration card with correct information. After visiting you, they check their email inbox. **Nothing.** They check their phone messages. **Nothing.**

Shopper "A" is an ideal customer. I can't imagine what would happen if a B-shopper came in, which mirrors what salespeople usually see onsite. Prospects come in and they haven't sold their home yet, they're not with their spouse, they just started looking, etc. If "A" prospects are not followed up properly, forget about getting results with B's or C's.

OUTSTANDING FOLLOW UP GIVES YOU A COMPETITIVE EDGE

The three very different examples of follow up letters below show you how to make a lasting impression and impact.

TIE KEY POINTS TO HOME FEATURES

Reconfirming that the home is suitable to their needs today and tomorrow is the focus of this example:

Dear Patty:

I would like to thank you once again for visiting our Bellagio community this morning. It was such a pleasure meeting and speaking with you. I've attached the option selection catalog for the Tuscany II home for your review as well as the survey (with a house on it) for home site #1718.

The home seems like a perfect fit for your family of five. Additionally, it has plenty of space for them to grow up in and the back yard is ideal for sports and barbecues.

I will contact you in a couple of days after you've had a chance to review this information. I'm sure our community will be a grea+t fit for you and your family. Have a great day!

Sincerely,

Nancy

Sales Agent

Fantastic Follow Up Finale

In my seminars through the years, I've always discussed "quirky" and unusual types of follow up that will break through the boring clutter and get noticed. At minimum, my theory is if everyone is emailing, you should send snail mail or call. But being really different will definitely make you stand out from the crowd.

Dear Fido,

Thanks for bringing your owners to see us at ABC Homes today. I hope you liked the doggie biscuits and your owners can get more treats for you with the enclosed PetSmart gift certificate. There's a PetSmart one mile from our community in addition to a super doggie park, doggie day care, and Miss Emily's Bed and Biscuit (the coolest boarding place in "your" city). I will follow up shortly with your owners to come visit us again and bring you along. We have treats!

Paws to you,

Nancy

Sales Agent

WRITE TO THE FAMILY PET

An example of quirky would be to follow up with Fido, as shown in the previous example. Yup. Find out the name of the prospect's pet and send a follow up to their pet!

You have to admit if you received a follow up letter like this one, you'd be impressed!

WRITE TO THE CHILDREN

Another follow up idea is to send a letter directly to the children in the family, as shown in the Dear Little Patty Prospect example on page 97. If you win over the hearts of the kids, that's the deciding factor for mom and dad to make the move in some instances.

BE CRAFTY AND CREATIVE

Another clever, low cost follow up idea is to go to your nearby crafts store and purchase some small 3" X 3" fences. Buy padded envelopes and insert the fencing along with your personalized letter to remind your prospects it's "time to get off the fence" as prices are going to be increasing.

Your follow up campaign should consist of items of interest to the prospect that were discussed during the visit. For example, if

---

Dear Little Patty Prospect,

Thanks for bringing your parents to visit ABC Homes. I think the "pink princess" room has your name on it. The loft area upstairs would be perfect for sleepovers and you won't bother mom and dad who are on the other side of the house. I've enclosed some information about the local riding stables that the kids here say are "awesome." I will follow up again soon to see when you and your family can make a second visit.

Sincerely,

Nancy

Sales Agent

---

they mentioned a passion for hiking, send them a trail map of the local hikes at area parks. If they're interested in working out, send them information on various gyms in your area.

Develop your follow up plan as soon as the prospect leaves your sales center. Use the notes you made during the presentation to design something unique. As you can see, the more you were able to get to know your prospects, the more customized and personalized your follow up can be.

> **TIP:** In your follow up, become a resource, not another pesky salesperson. Be creative like the examples to keep your name top of the mind and continue working the sales process to seal the deal. Whatever you do, always include a "call to action."

PERSEVERE POLITELY TO SCHEDULE THE RETURN VISIT

It's vital to continue to follow up with the end goal in mind: setting an appointment for a return visit. Set an automated reminder in your calendar for the follow up task at hand. When you perform the reminder, don't use a boring form letter message.

It's also important to continually reclassify your prospects throughout the sales process. For example, a "C" prospect can jump to "A" status if they sold their home.

The follow up requires you to use your imagination and get creative. If you zero in on what's most important to your prospects and become a valuable resource, I promise you they'll be delighted to take your follow up call.

CHAPTER 11

Would You Buy A Home From You?

The SA wore a too-tight glittery tank top with bra straps exposed, flip flops, and jeans. Her cleavage was a distraction. Her long hair was teased out to the max! She looked more like she was dressed to go "clubbing" than to conduct a sales presentation. Even though she was extremely knowledgeable in her presentation, her clothing and appearance were distracting and took away from her overall credibility.

It's no secret that people buy from someone they like and trust. As an SA, your main focus is to be likeable and professional at all times. Part of these qualities is being upbeat and enthusiastic. Sure, it can get tough day in and day out, but think of actors on Broadway who do the same show every day multiple times a day. Adapt their mindset. Tourists flock to New York's theater district, paying over $100 a ticket to see a Broadway show. Can you imagine the actors coming out tired, not very peppy, and messing up their lines? The same concept holds true in new home sales centers. You're an actor, every prospect is a new "audience," and even if you don't feel upbeat, you must act as if you are.

Here are the questions evaluating the SA's appearance and demeanor from the shopping report:

- Did the SA appear energetic and enthusiastic?
- Did the SA demonstrate a professional, courteous, friendly demeanor?
- Did the SA have an organized presentation?
- Did the SA seem in control of the sales process?
- Did the SA listen well?
- Did the SA attempt to build rapport with the prospect?
- Did the SA have good product knowledge?

- Did the SA handle traffic well (i.e. multiple prospects, other visitors, etc.)?
- Did the SA handle interruptions well (i.e. phone calls)?
- Did the SA seem genuinely interested in the prospect?

The following comments from mystery shops are exactly what **not** to do:

....

The SA took 3 cell phone calls while we toured the model.

....

The SA did not know the area well, was unaware of several option prices, and kept saying "I'm new here and will need to get these answers for you."

....

The SA showed me eight different plans for a three bedroom, and took over 30 minutes to narrow down to a plan that would work well in my budget.

....

I walked in wanting to build a two story, three bedroom with a bonus room plan. The SA kept pushing the inventory home which was one story and too small for my family.

....

Delving into detail on some of the questions in the shopping report will help you fine tune "you."

DID THE SA APPEAR ENERGETIC AND ENTHUSIASTIC?

Close your eyes. I mean it. Close your eyes. Visualize either Brad Pitt or Angelina Jolie, whichever you dream about meeting. Next, imagine yourself seeing the one you picked walk up to your sales center. Would you be excited? Would you jump out of your chair and put some enthusiasm in your step? Of course you would! Even if it was 6:00 pm and you were closing up for the day? Of course you would!

This is the "state of mind" you need to be in for every prospect. Every prospect should be treated just as you would treat Brad Pitt and/or Angelina Jolie. I can promise that this one modification will boost your sales up, up, up. Simply put, you'll sell more homes if you show more energy and enthusiasm.

I know it's challenging at the end of the day or after a long week of tire kickers and prospects who don't qualify. Enthusiasm tends to disappear and you're just going through the motions. The tour sounds very robotic and canned because you've said the same thing hundreds of times. The key is to remember that for the prospect walking in, today is the first time they're seeing your gorgeous models, your incredible landscaping, your state of the art fitness center, your beautiful community center, etc.

102

> **TIP:** Focus on "helping" and "serving" your prospects and take the focus off yourself. Your enthusiasm and energy will come naturally…and sales will roll in.

Here's an idea to consider: Change one word. Change *"got"* to *"get."* I'll explain…

A few years ago, I attended my local chapter meeting of the National Association of Speakers. Ray Pelletier was the presenter and he was awesome. I volunteered to drive Ray back to the airport. He asked me what I speak on, where I travel to, etc.

"I present to the home building industry and I've *got* to go to Toronto next week to give a talk," I told him.

Ray stared at me and said. "You've *got* to go?"

I replied, "Yeah, I've *got* to fly in the night before, meet with some members of the local HBA, then speak the next morning."

Ray asked, "Are they paying your travel?"

"Yes," I said.

He continued. "Are they putting you up in a nice hotel and taking you out for dinner?"

"Uh huh."

"Are they paying your speaking fee?"

"Yes." I was starting to see where this was going.

"Well, my dear, you *get* to go to Toronto", said Ray. "Think of how many beginner speakers would kill to be in your shoes, travelling out of the country, having all their expenses paid, and earn their full speaking fee."

Some of you are likely thinking to yourself, "I've *got* to work some numbers to help the Smiths get qualified for the home they liked" or "I've *got* to do more follow up and bring in more traffic."

Just like Ray told me, here is the change you also need to make, "If you just change that one word *'got'* to *'get,'* your entire approach will change."

The reward of being an SA is you *get* to help prospects move into a gorgeous new home that will change their lives!

DID THE SA DEMONSTRATE A PROFESSIONAL, COURTEOUS, FRIENDLY DEMEANOR?

Imagine walking into your local bank. You're doing really well lately and you want to open a new CD or money market account. The bank president appears wearing shorts, flip flops, and a Hawaiian shirt with coffee stains. How confident would you be giving this bank your money?

> **TIP:** Professional business attire is a must to develop the trust and confidence of prospects. Always dress professionally and appropriately. The focus should be on your model homes, not you. Here's a simple test: Before going to work each morning, look in the mirror and ask yourself, "Would I buy a home from me?"

Do you recall news reports a few years back when a group of college girls wearing flip flops went to visit President George W. Bush? Not impressive, to say the least.

I personally see travelers on planes wearing pajamas and slippers. It's disgraceful.

Many builders don't have a dress code in place and don't offer any guidance to the sales team on "appropriate dress" for the sales centers. It's up to you to present the most professional image possible.

DID THE SA LISTEN WELL?

My entire 2012 Super Sales Rally speech at the International Builders Show was on "listening." After watching thousands of video mystery shops, I was seeing the same pattern over and over. SA's were talking far too much, not asking enough questions, and *not* really listening. What you have to say is much more impactful if you've spent more time listening than talking.

Before my mom passed away, she lived at a nearby assisted living community and I visited her every day. I would walk in and see her in the lobby. She looked half asleep but when she saw me, her eyes would light up and she would always say the same thing, "Have a seat, Melinda. You talk, I'll listen." It made me feel incredibly special.

Imagine if we said those words to our prospects as they walked into the sales center: "You talk, I'll listen."

How many times have you been in a sales environment and felt everything *but* listened to?

The majority of our mystery shops reveal the sales person talking most of the time...

"Let me tell you all about the community..."
"Let me tell you all about our floor plans..."
"Let me tell you all about the builder..."

It's like having all this information and throwing it up all over the prospect!

On Oprah's last show, she said, "I've talked to nearly 30,000 people on this show and all 30,000 had one thing in common. They all wanted validation." Validation means, "I hear *you*." "I care

> **TIP:** Have a dialogue, not a monologue with each prospect. Ask a few questions. Be quiet and really listen for the response. Gradually probe deeper. Ask why something is important or why it's an issue. Listen, listen, listen. Then address the concerns and check in again with the prospect.

about what *you* have to say." Validate your prospects by zeroing in on what they've specifically said. Be comfortable with silence and the pauses.

DID THE SA ATTEMPT TO BUILD RAPPORT WITH THE PROSPECT?

The process of building trust and rapport starts from the second a prospect sees you. It continues throughout the entire selling process. Your job is to be likeable. This can be challenging because prospects often try to avoid you when they first walk in the sales center. They have a preconceived notion that you're the "big bad, pushy salesperson" and they prefer to do their own thing and look around.

Here are excellent examples of building rapport....

....

The SA developed great rapport with us. She asked where we were moving from and when we said, "Raleigh," she told us she had lived there, so we compared notes about the area. She was professional, knowledgeable, and very tuned into our needs. Her phone rang twice and she ignored it and gave us her full attention.

....

The SA truly listened to the prospect when she mentioned her concern about the schools. The SA empathized and suggested a tour of the school and meeting with the principal.

....

TIP: People do business with you when they know, like, and trust you. The way to connect and develop a relationship with your prospect is to build trust and rapport. The easiest way to connect with a prospect is to quickly find some common ground.

CHAPTER 12

The Surprise Ending

And now for the "rest of the story"......Remember the opening story I shared with you in Chapter 1, "I Can Identify With You," recalling when, in 1977, I was mystery shopped by Ron Hall, the vice president of the company that managed the property I worked for? You know, the one I not only flunked but "earned" a negative 2 score? I moved on from that firm, and the next company, Johnstown American, offered a ton of sales training. They flew sales agents to Atlanta for week- long classes on qualifying, demonstrating, closing, etc. We role played, brainstormed, and practiced throughout the entire week. At the community where I worked, every week we had sales meetings which were always training oriented.

I returned from the Atlanta training and became a "closing machine." The UPS guy, the mailman, anyone within 10 yards of me was going to be closed...watch out!

TIP: Sales managers reading this...Hire apartment leasing agents for your new home communities. They're **very** well trained, are willing to work long hours and weekends, and will appreciate the income opportunity of new home sales.

That's not the end though. Fast forward from 1977 to 11 years later, 1986, when I founded Melinda Brody and Company. I received a call from Ron Hall. Yes, the same Ron Hall who is forever embedded in my memory. He was now in Kalamazoo, Michigan, operating a company that leased apartments and sold condominiums. He told me he heard of my company and wanted to fly me in to present a full-day seminar to his sales staff. Wow! Should I tell him? Nah, I think I'll keep the shopping experience my little secret.

Ron flew me out to Kalamazoo, paid my full speaking fee plus expenses – and it was great. Fifty people were at the program and they gave me excellent marks in their feedback. Ron took me to the airport. On the way, I couldn't control myself.

"Ron," I said. "Do you remember me? Do I look familiar?"

"No," he answered.

"Sandy Cove Apartments. July 1977. You shopped me and I did awful."

He looked at me puzzled.

Ever so nonchalantly, Ron said, "You know, Melinda, I don't remember that but I'm glad I helped you on your career path."

Words of Gold.

I hope that by reading *"They Said What??!!,"* I've paid it forward and put you on a more exciting and rewarding career path in new home sales!

CHAPTER 13

Bonus Stories

(Author's Note: I didn't make this stuff up!!!!!)

....

SA did terrible on his shop and he knew it. He called our shopper and asked if he could erase the tape and come back in so he could do the entire sales presentation over.

....

SA went into her personal issues about being homeless, losing her house, car, etc., and then having multiple medical problems.

....

"It's been extremely slow."

....

"The market is bad."

....

Took phone call and discussed something is "pretty well infested."

....

The builder didn't have a model but instead, there was a sales center. The SA, a male perhaps in his 40's, was an affable sort of fellow. I couldn't help but notice that he was somewhat disheveled looking. He had a three-day growth of beard and some sort of skin condition on his neck. He wore green pants and an orange shirt...not your typical looking SA. He gave a presentation and then invited me to sit down across the desk from him. During the course of our conversation, he asked me what kind of work I do. I replied that I was a pharmacist for the new Walgreens that had just opened nearby. He made comments about how he wished that he was a pharmacist. He said he would put balloons up in front of the security camera and grab some drugs for himself. He did a poor job of selling. I don't know if he had a job after that.

....

I was going to do a shop at a townhome. The instructions indicated that the SA was a female. As I walked in the front door, I could see a wide open door down the hall and I could hear what I thought was water running. I stood there for a moment wondering if I should proceed. It was at that point that I heard a toilet flush. Was the situation what I thought it might be? The female SA came out from the powder room and was surprised to see me standing in the foyer. Her face was red. I'll bet she started shutting the door after that!

....

The shop instructions indicated that there would be a female SA in a sales center, no model. The SA seemed very friendly and enthusiastic, perhaps overly so. During her presentation, she offered me cookies. I declined the cookies and said "thank you." Her reply was, "I will bake cookies for you anytime." I'm a little naïve about such advances so the comment went over my head. As we were nearing the end of our conversation about the homes, the SA suggested that I come back for a second look. I asked her what days she was there. She told me, "Well, there are seven days in a week and I have a cot in the back room." I realized at that point what was going on!

....

When doing a shop with my daughter, we ran into a SA that was having what must have been a bad day. We walked into the sales area and found the female SA was sitting at the desk looking at her computer. She barely acknowledged that we were there much less showing any interest in selling us a home. I told her we would like some information on the homes. She pointed to a price list on a table across the room and then went back to whatever she was doing. We looked at the model by ourselves and when we returned, attempted to engage the SA. She was still sitting there looking disgruntled about something and showed no interest in selling. After asking her questions to show our interest, it was obvious she had no interest in selling. End of shop.

....

I was given specific instructions from the homebuilder/client about information that I might be able to get during this shop. Since the

*homes were selling like hotcakes, it was rumored that the SA was flip-
ping homes for buyers. That is, she would sell a home to the original
buyer then turn around and resell it to another buyer at a higher
price taking a commission on the resale "under the table." It took only
seven minutes to figure this out!*

....

*During the tour of an inventory home, the SA pointed out the lovely
wood railing on the steps leading to the second story of the home. The
home was still in the finishing stages and a small bag of wooden "buttons" was attached to the railing which workers would use to cover the
nail heads. The SA commented, "I need some of these at home!" and
proceeded to empty a handful of the buttons from the bag and put
them in his pocket.*

....

*Shoppers were told "The directions on the website are wrong and
people are constantly calling me...."*

....

*The male SA greeted me by commenting how much he liked the
blouse I was wearing and how good I looked in that color. He continued to compliment me throughout the tour of the model and
the community. When we returned to the sales office, he asked if
I would like to see his dog, which he brought out for me to pet. Finally, instead of attempting to "close," he said he really didn't think I
belonged in his community (not nice enough) and suggested I check
out the competition.*

....

The SA wanted to take me to see the inventory homes. We decided to take her car but when I got in the car, there was a pedal by my feet on the passenger floor. I started to laugh and the SA said, "OMG, I am so sorry. This is my husband's driving school car and I had to use it today." The SA told me not to put my foot on the pedal or we would go flying. I was laughing so hard that I said, "Don't worry, my feet are going to be so far from that pedal that I'm going to sit cross-legged so I'm not even close to the pedal." I had the SA laughing so hard!

....

The SA greeted me and started to talk about my Harley necklace and how he had a Harley motorcycle. The SA told me the entire story about his motorcycles, his grandson, and showed me pictures of his wife. The SA never asked me about homes. When we finally started to discuss what kind of home I wanted, the SA's cell phone rang six times within 15 minutes and he answered every call and talked to each person on the phone. He still never talked to me about the homes. After I finally got his attention on the homes, the SA began to explain a new home that he just designed and he wanted to take me to the lot. As we drove to the lot, the SA told me who lived in every home and what they did for a living. When we got to the lot, the SA showed me where the house was going to sit and the lake. The SA started to tell me about his life and how he was the best engineer in the company and he lived all over the world and would be called to fix all the problems since he was the best! By the time we got back to the office, I knew nothing about the company, nothing about the homes, was never asked about what I was looking for. All I knew about this location was all about the SA. Oh, the best part of the story...the SA had plaques on the wall nominating him for Best Sales Associate of the Year! He was the Best BS Artist I've ever seen!

....

SA: "What do you do?"

Shopper: "I work for AT&T."

SA: "I had dropped calls from AT&T today. They drop calls a lot. Do you have that problem?"

....

The SA noticed an email from the sales manager while with our shopper and said, "I wonder what the SOB wants now." After reading the email, he then complained about having to go to a sales meeting with a motivational speaker, saying "I'm 66 years old, I don't need this." Later on, as the shopper was leaving, the SA said, "Just call me on my cell phone because when you call in the office number, they tape the calls to check on us. I hate that."

....

As the SA pointed out the downspouts and gutters in the pool area, he backed himself into the pool. Although soaking wet, he continued on with his presentation. The builder who hired us gave cash rewards for top shop scores. This SA was given flippers and goggles!

....

APPENDIX

Chapter Challenges

These exercises, designed for both sales agents and sales managers, correspond with concepts presented in each chapter of *"They Said What??!!"* Use these Chapter Challenges frequently to become more proficient in every part of the sales process and make your sales soar.

CHAPTER 2: YOU HAD ME AT HELLO

Sales Agent: When you attend a networking event, realtor function, or personal party, challenge yourself to really listen and focus on people's names. See how many you can remember. I guarantee you will be one of the few who can do this successfully!

Sales Manager: The "Name Game" is a great memory exercise. Far too often sales associates don't use their prospect's name (or prospects' names) during the presentation. In many cases it's because they can't remember it and are embarrassed to ask again. Using your prospect's name throughout the presentation is critical in developing rapport. Teach your sales team how to memorize their customer's name with a word association game. Assign fake names to each member of the team. The first person stands, announces her name and something that she likes that happens to start with the same letter as her first name. For example: "I'm Marcia and I like motorcycles." The second person follows suit but also repeats what the first person said. This continues around the room until the last person tries to repeat the names of every person in the room along with their matching interest. This game emphasizes listening, repetition, and focus — and it's fun to play!

CHAPTER 3: GETTING TO KNOW YOU

Sales Agent: For the next 30 days, make a list of all traffic that visits your sales center. Write down every customer's hobbies and interests. How many people are in their family? What are the names of their children? Are you struggling? Make it a personal goal to be mindful moving forward to collect this information and make notes about it .

Sales Manager: Help your team shift from a product to prospect driven presentation. On index cards, have the team write a "back story" for a fictitious customer. Why are they moving? Are they renting or in a home that's sold? How many are in the family, names, ages, pets, etc.? Must haves in a home, time frame, price range, etc.? Have the SA's match up. One is the SA and one is the customer. The customer needs to follow the back story written on the index card. The SA practices getting the information from them in a smooth, conversational manner.

Here's another idea called the "Empty Chair" exercise. At an upcoming sales meeting, leave one chair empty and explain that this represents the customer. If they were present, how would they feel about decisions made? What's going through their mind? What are their wants and needs? Jeff Bezos of Amazon.com has done this for years. He only happens to be one of the wealthiest 35 people on the planet!

CHAPTER 4: WHO CARES ABOUT THE CLUBHOUSE!

Sales Agent: Write a list of 25 amazing things about your community.

Sales Manager: Develop a "Community Quiz" for an upcoming sales meeting. Questions can be:

- Name of area day care?
- Name of area dry cleaners?
- Name of area Catholic church, etc.?
- Name of the local high school principal?
- Name of local park?

Give a prize to the sales person who has the most product knowledge about the surrounding community.

CHAPTER 5: WE ARE A QUALITY BUILDER (SNOOZE)

Sales Agent: Think of some companies that are standouts in their industry. Southwest Airlines, Disney, and Harley Davidson come to my mind. Read "Category of One" by Joe Calloway. Begin to craft your builder's story using the Unique Selling Proposition/USP and fill in the blanks in this statement, "We are the only builder in _____ who_____."

Sales Manager: Have each SA bring in their builder story and discuss them as a team. Have the SA's brainstorm and write one that everyone will use. Make it unique, compelling, and different.

CHAPTER 6: WALK THIS WAY

Sales Agent: Go through three popular floor plans and in each room, write down the benefits, where you would stand when touring, and the way other buyers have utilized the space.

Sales Manager: This practice exercise will get the sales team comfortable with "benefit selling." Gather a variety of objects (stuffed animal, large paper clip, back scratcher, candy bar, etc.) and drop them in a box. At your next sales meeting, each SA pulls out an object without looking. Tell them they're now going to sell the object to the rest of the team but they can only talk in terms of benefits, not features. Watch and listen how challenging this is!

CHAPTER 7: DEMO THE DIRT

Sales Agent: Pick three locations and write down all the benefits of that location, where to stand when demonstrating it, and suggestions on how other buyers have used the home site (pools, patios, gardens, swing sets, etc.).

Sales Manager: To practice demonstrating the location, do you have an available (express) home that's been sitting for awhile? Have your next sales meeting in the home and brainstorm all the benefits of the home with your team.

CHAPTER 8: YOU CAN'T HANDLE THE TRUTH (OR OBJECTIONS)

Sales Agent: Develop an objection list of your top 10 objections heard from prospects, i.e., "too far out"; "lot too small"; "too expensive"; "not enough closets," etc. Write a solid planned answer to each objection. Keep the information on your smart phone or tablet and review it each day when you open your model center.

Sales Manager: Bring some throw pillows to your sales meeting. Have each SA write down the top three objections they hear from prospects. Role play these objections by giving the SA a throw pillow. As the "customer" voices the objection, have the SA toss the pillow to them as a visual of "softening" the objection and practicing the magic words, "I understand…" This is a great visual reminder to use empathy when dealing with objections.

CHAPTER 9: LET'S WRAP THINGS UP

Sales Agent: Purchase John Palumbo's series of books on becoming a "master closer." He's **the** expert. (www.JohnPalumbo.com)

Sales Manager: To have your team practice handling rejection, everyone stands up simultaneously and approaches someone in the room and asks for the sale. Whoever is asked for the sale, must answer "no." The one who asked says "thanks" and moves on. Debrief the group and inquire, "How did that feel"? Emphasize with them, "The world didn't stop. You didn't die. You weren't despised." Next, repeat the "buy now" activity and when asked, the response will always be "yes." Debrief again. Ask the group "How did that feel?" To begin to excel at being a closer, the sales team has to be comfortable asking everyone for a commitment and handling the answer. Remind them, "If you don't ask, the answer is always "no"!

CHAPTER 10: FANTASTIC FOLLOW UP FINALE

Sales Agent: Bring in three examples of creative follow up that you've received as a prospect.

Sales Manager: Challenge the sales team to develop a creative follow up campaign with their prospects. Have them bring three examples of follow up ideas to send that are unusual, quirky, and innovative. Have the sales team vote on the top three ideas.

CHAPTER 11: WOULD YOU BUY A HOME FROM YOU!

Sales Agent: Take notice of how professional people act and look when you're the prospect in a bank, at a store, at a doctor's office. What's an amazing first impression when you're in the prospect role? What do they do that would be fitting for you as an SA? Do it!

Sales Manager: Here's a "common ground" exercise. Have the team break into small groups of three to four people. Set a timer for five minutes. In that time span, everyone has to find common ground between them and it needs to be things that are simple but not obvious. Simple would be "We've all been to Europe." Obvious would be "We're all wearing blue" or "We're all sales people." This will reinforce how common ground bonds and connects people, which is an essential element in sales success.

ACKNOWLEDGEMENTS

I'm grateful to be part of three Mastermind groups which continue to guide me on my career path by giving me brutally honest feedback on improvements and shortcomings as well as cheer on my successes. In no particular order, thank you John Palumbo, Meredith Oliver, Becky Nickol, Judith Dacey, Rick Bommelje, Carl Chauncey, Denise Messineo, Karen Brandell, J.B. Adams, Armie Payas, Ann Newhouse, and Pat McLeod.

Many incredible people have been a part of The Melinda Brody Team over the years. Thank you to Kim French, Director of Client Services and my right hand. Also, I extend my deepest appreciation to Marilyn Whelan, my partner in the beginning of my company, for her guidance and optimistic attitude, and Lisa Baez for her invaluable contribution during her years as Director of Operations. Others who've been instrumental in always making me look good include Jeanne Brancheau, Karen Marsh, Leanne Douglass, Misty Rodriguez, Julie Passmore, Rod Eddins, Sandy O'Connell, and Leah Turner.

Thanks to all of the video mystery shoppers who contributed stories to this book and who will forever remain "mysterious."

I had terrific support, guidance, and creativity from Jerry Dorris, my book designer, and Sheryl Kurland, my editor.

Nothing would be possible without the love and support of my entrepreneurial friends/sisters — Ruth Stern, Nancy Holman, Sarah Thomas, Rosario Ortigao, Bobbe Lyon, and Karen Madanick.

I'm lucky to have the support of my loving partner, Howard Kemp, and my amazing daughter, Sarah Brody.

ABOUT THE AUTHOR

Melinda Brody is president of Melinda Brody and Company, Inc. For three decades, Melinda's firm has video mystery shopped over 25,000 onsite salespeople and knows what's *REALLY* going on in the field of new home sales. Melinda is a member of the Institute of Residential Marketing and has spoken at the International Builders' Show dozens of times. She is a regular featured speaker at the popular Super Sales Rally. In addition to video mystery shopping, Melinda's firm offers sales training, keynote speaking, sales coaching with the shops, and training DVD's. Melinda is a member of the National Speakers Association and the Mystery Shopping Providers Association.

CONNECT WITH MELINDA

sell@melindabrody.com

407-294-7614 ext. 301

www.MelindaBrody.com

Facebook.com/MelindaBrody

Linkedin/Melinda Brody

YouTube/VideoShoppingTV

Twitter/Melinda407

Blog: wordpress.com/MelindaBrody

DISCOUNT AVAILABLE
ORDER IN QUANTITY FOR YOUR SALES TEAM

If you would like to order multiple copies of *"They Said WHAT??!!,"* we offer a quantity discount.

Please email us at <u>sell@melindabrody.com</u>

or call 407-294-7614 ext. 301.

Made in the USA
Charleston, SC
29 July 2013